416-899-1264

The Essential

EVITA BEZUIDENHOUT

compiled by
Pieter-Dirk Uys

DAVID PHILIP PUBLISHERS
Cape Town

First published 1997 in southern Africa by David Philip Publishers (Pty) Ltd, 208 Werdmuller Centre, Claremont 7700

ISBN 0-86486-349-7

© 1997 Pieter-Dirk Uys 1997

All rights reserved

Printed in South Africa by National Book Printers, Drukkery Street, Goodwood Western Cape

Evita Bezuidenhout

Born Evangelie Poggenpoel of humble Boer origins in the dusty Orange Free State town of Bethlehem in 1935, on 28th September. Illegitimate, talented, beautiful and ambitious, she dreams of fame and fortune, tasting it as the star of such '50s Afrikaner film classics as 'Boggel en die Akkedis' (Hunchback and the Lizard), 'Meisie van my Drome' (Girl of my Dreams) and 'Duiwelsvallei' (Devil's Valley). Marries into the political Bezuidenhout dynasty and becomes the demure wife of Member of Parliament Dr J.J. de V. Bezuidenhout and the mother of three. Power becomes her addiction. She wields it in the bedroom, the kitchen, and round the dinner table, becoming confidante to the gods on the Boere Olympus, and shaping the course of history with her close and often shocking relationships with the grim-faced leaders of the day: Dr Hendrik F. Verwoerd, the Architect of Apartheid and the father figure she never knew; Balthazar John Vorster, the ruthless policeman of the ruling National Party, at the same time her mortal enemy and closet admirer; P.W. Botha, the explosive Caesar of change and reform, the Napoleon to her Madame de Staël; F.W. de Klerk, the urbane and pleasing designer-politician, who took her advice, smiled and set the land on a new course. Hand in hand with the glamorous Evita of Pretoria is the Talleyrand of Africa, Foreign Minister Pik Botha, her ageing Romeo and friend; while watching her from afar, as she watched him, is Nelson Mandela, alive today only thanks to her timely intervention. And as the former barefoot girl from Bethlehem majestically sails into the stormy seas of her marriage and her maturity, dazzling friend and foe alike with her authority and dreaded irony, like any other educated white South African she constantly passes by the terrible aftermath of the apartheid system she helped spawn and, having seen, looks away at her smiling reflection in the pools of blood at her feet.

Today's most famous white woman in South Africa, Evita Bezuidenhout seems to have steered her ship of survival through the stormy swells of radical change like an explorer of old. She will probably be one of the few true Afrikaner aristocrats not to have lost her head on the tumbrils of democracy. As retired SA Ambassador to the former black homeland of Bapetikosweti, Mrs Bezuidenhout is the Official Afrikaans Substitute First Lady to President Nelson Mandela. There are also rumours that she might be asked to lead the National Party in the 1999 elections.

Mrs Bezuidenhout is now an honorary member of the ANC Women's League, where she is known as 'Comrade iVita b'Zuidenhout'. She was the chairperson of OLYMPICS FOR CAPE TOWN (OLFOCT).

On Thursday 26th October 1995, Mrs Evita Bezuidenhout, accompanied by the Speaker of Parliament, Dr Frene Ginwala, attended the unveiling of a bust of the former Ambassador in the foyer of the former House of Assembly. It was attended by members of the media and of Parliament.

Apartheid It is only fair to start the *Essential Evita* with a definition of the thing that has made me famous, or infamous, depending which side you're on. Apartheid was most definitely not 'a pigment of the imagination' as someone once wrote on the wall of the men's toilet in Parliament. (Pik told me!) It is difficult to recall its attraction in this time of instant democracy. Officially now apartheid is dead, but the memory lingers on like a dead rat under the cathedral floorboards. It was for most of my life not so much a policy, more a way of existence. Liberals see it as a sly political game of ethnic scrabble, in which the whites won everything without trying, and the blacks cleaned up afterwards without choice.

If you were white, living in Johannesburg, and knew that for each of you there were ten of them, apartheid wasn't such an easy thing to ignore. But it will always have a very simple obituary in all eleven languages: never again! Never again on paper! Never again in law! We Afrikaners are really so silly. We put apartheid in the statute books and look what happened? No one ever put the word 'Prejudice' on a T-shirt? Why, they even make films about Pride and Prejudice today…

Afrikaans The most beautiful language to have been made up in 15 minutes! More a dialect of Dutch than the Flemish language is today. Reputed to have been what Dutch sounded like in 1652. Apartheid politics demanded its official enshrinement as the 'youngest language in the world'! Originally it was the most favoured 'taal' in which to arrest thousands of blacks. Also to say 'voertsek' to the world. Afrikaans must now take its place quite far down the line of official languages in South Africa. Once one of the only two Linguae Africanae (the other being English), the future of Afrikaans looks either bright or dire, depending where you view it from. If finally freed of the baggage of bad politics, Afrikaans could thrive and bloom. If used as a shield behind which to wage an ethnic civil war, it will soon vanish off the battlefield, if not the toilet walls. Afrikaans is still young enough to recover its common sense after being molested as a 'taal slaaf' (a language slave) by the Nationalist Government.

ANC Used to stand for African National Congress and is our present government in action, after being a government in exile for so many comfortable years while fighting The Struggle (see *Struggle*). It stepped into the warm slippers of power from the Moral High Ground (see under *M*) that has been quickly levelled to a morass through expected corruption and carelessness. ANC can also stand for A Nice Cheque, as it has become the best government money can buy (see *Taiwan*). Large sums have been paid the party to aid 'its struggle against apartheid', but also to nudge it away from criticising the leaders of Nigeria for hanging opponents, or to lure it away from diplomatic recognitions of unfashionable states (see *Taiwan*). Now longing for the good old days of opposition, the ANC has never had to rule a real country, or take any responsibility for its actions. Then it could always blame apartheid. It still does. When will someone tell them? The buck stops at the gates of power. Will the ANC acknowledge it? Or just eat the buck and turn its skin into yet another traditional cultural outfit? (See *Buthelezi*)

AWB This stands for Afrikaner Weerstandsbeweging, or Afrikaner Resistance Movement, where there is little resistance and absolutely no movement. A small minor grouping of eccentric overweight old-fashioned former Nats, who have found an easy way to free publicity on overseas TV by wearing funny hats, growing dirty beards, falling drunk off their horses while waving sloppy Nazi salutes. They still pretend to represent a nation at war, but probably have as their members a dozen senile ex-policemen fired for molesting sheep and drunken driving; a few ex-Rhodesians who aren't very good at keeping countries (see *Rhodesia*); and a few disappointed Brits who emigrated to South Africa to share in the glories of apartheid, but got here too late for cheap maids and garden boys. Led by a fat man called Eugene TerreBlanche who has holes in his green Y-fronts and cries on the witness stand.

AIDS Not Foreign Aids; something more easily spread. Afrikaners can't get it, because we're not black, we don't take drugs and we are not sexually experimental. But my son De Kock says that this horrible AIDS is the only truly democratic thing left in the world today. It doesn't take sides; anyone can get it! (Except Afrikaners!) So De Kock has told me to tell you to: Put your Love in a Plastic Bag!

Affirmative Action A radical way to rebalance a badly listing ship of state. To a civil service top-heavy with Bothas,

De Villierses, Van der Merwes, Steyns and Smits, add an equal number of Mzibukos, Mbathas, Nkosis, Khumalos and Zwanes. A necessary process of bending over blackwards. Early retirement and lavish golden handshakes will see a departure of some Bothas, De Villierses, Van der Merwes, Steyns and Smits. The ship of state will sink back into a familiar list, this time to the left.

AK47 A machine gun, cheaper to buy in South Africa today than the latest Wilbur Smith novel in hardcover.

Afrikaner Finally to be condemned to a footnote in the history books: 'Afrikaners: a white tribe of basically decent people who went mad on the Southern Tip of Africa and had eventually to be put to sleep in the most humane way.' Democratically, of course! A new breed of Afrikaner is emerging: not white, not Calvinist, not chosen, just needed at the voting booth in order to keep old white chauvinist chosen Afrikaners still in power (see *Western Cape*).

Amandla The cry of liberation, meaning Freedom. A Xhosa translation of the Afrikaans word 'Vrystaat!'

Aia Another Afrikaans word that is untranslatable: it probably means 'nanny', but that's so feeble. Aia was the person who was there in the dark when you were frightened. Aia took you to school. Aia was always big and fat and barefoot. Aia was the substitute mother you always fell asleep against and the maid you never had to apologise to. Aia is now unionised and goes on strike if you call her that. Today you call Aia 'Ms. Comrade'.

Bill of Rights A list of things you can expect to get away with in a normal society. South Africa will never be that, so ordinary things like life have to be protected. It's a wonderful thing to brag about at dinner parties in the UK, where they do not have a Bill of Rights. The right to life is one thing; the right to live like a parasite is another. I feel the less rights we guarantee, the more rights we have to earn. Call me old-fashioned.

Bantustans An ornate word to describe what was known as the Homelands, before the concept of Bantu became Plural, then became Angry, which became Black, which became Beautiful. Dr Verwoerd had this dream to divide South Africa equally into different states: white states and black states. The black states would be known as Bantustans, while the white state would be South Africa. It nearly went beyond the point of no return. First Bantustan was Transkei. Then Ciskei became the second Xhosa homeland, underlining the concept of divide to rule! Then all those 8 pieces of Bophuthatswana, with Sun City as the paste jewel in its crown. Followed by my Bapetikosweti, with Venda and so on. Bantustans gave many whites a chance to be human. Our people could go there and gamble, which was illegal in South Africa. They could see rude films, also illegal back home. Even sleep with blacks and not be arrested, which was impossible across the border! But you didn't need a passport to cross into the Homelands; just a valid Visa card. They are now as rare as elephants singing a cappella on CD. The 'stan' part has been exported and lives on today in Uzbekistan, Afghanistan, Kazakhstan, Pakistan and a whole cluster of Otherstans who, like our own stans, all want a flag, a civil war, a casino and a special programme on CNN. Now there are no more Bantustans. Just one black Homeland: South Africa!

Boer The Afrikaans word for Farmer, but much more. The word Boer described my tribe. Remember, once the crux of democracy in South Africa was us one million whites, mainly Afrikaners, who voted the Government of the day into power, ignoring the thirtysomething million non-whites who couldn't. Boere, who were basically the Afrikaners who were farming, were paid huge subsidies to assist them in voting correctly. So wine farmers received millions of rands to develop grainlands that didn't exist; sheep farmers were paid as much to produce tobacco that wasn't there. Overnight this white security mist of Afrikaner/Boer rule dissolved in the glaring sun of a new democracy. Boere can now be found trekking north into foreign fields of Mozambique and Angola to try and find a hinterland there. Wine farmers will no doubt look for a sponsor in order to grow their tobacco.

Blacks Virtually everyone outside. They now rule South Africa, as there are officially 34 million of them, not counting the 5 million illegals, and still only 4 million of us whites. Till yesterday, that is. That's when the Cohens of Lower Houghton and the Van Zyls of Welkom emigrated. We were always taught that blacks were nice to you if you were strict with them. They were right; we were very strict with them. We put them in jail, we killed them, we kept them uneducated, we destroyed their families and look how nice they are to us today!

Boerestaat A joke. Rumours of a rightwing revolt simmer constantly. It's like promises of rain in a desert. There are still some old Afrikaners who want their separation from the world. They find it in different ways: some move to Johannesburg where from behind your eight-foot walls you never see anyone except muggers and hijackers. Some put their heads in the sand where they find many old friends also with their heads in the sand, having mislaid their bodies. And some diehards still want an independent white homeland. A Boerestaat. There is an official little one called Orangia. It is somewhere in the Northern Cape, windswept and barren. The reigning monarch is Mrs Betsie Verwoerd, widow of Hendrik (see *Verwoerd, Hendrik*). There is a statue of the architect of apartheid on the hill. The only intact statue of Verwoerd left in the world. It is very small. Takes me to my shoulders. When Nelson Mandela visited Betsie Verwoerd recently, he went to see the statue. 'They cut him down to size,' we think Mandela said.

Boesak, Allan The Reverend: Formerly ANC leader of the liberation movement in the Western Cape, having been a vibrant force in the UDF during the '80s. He lost the Province in the first 1994 election. We are so grateful, because the NP won instead! But Allan is too overtly ambitious, loudly Afrikaans, obviously coloured, officially religious and has a dangerously inflated ego and appetite for good food and blonde women. He also cannot count. Millions of Danish kroner in donations for the poor and needy vanished somewhere in his domain. As Allan is neither poor nor needy, we, the people, demand an explanation. Now he is threatening to put the Struggle on trial. Will it be The People versus Alan Boesak? Another O.J.Simpson farce? Maybe just an 'Oooo djay, Broeksak!'

Bobotie My favourite dish. I have conquered hearts and stomachs with my world-famous bobotie. In 1974 I was sent to New York to assist the SA Mission to the UN. Young Pik Botha was our new Ambassador. It was my first meeting with this remarkable man (see *Botha, Pik*). He suggested that I use my cooking arts to make friends for South Africa. Bobotie was the first attempt and Fiddle Castro was our first victim. He was in New York to make a speech at the UN. Because he was a hated communist, no one would feed him, or let him use their toilet. So we knew we had our first candidate. If he died, no one would care (see *Castro,*

Fiddle). But my bobotie was a great success and Fiddle complimented me. 'Evita, very good,' he said. I was so surprised he knew my name. But Pik told me, this Castro also had a girlfriend once called Evita, but she died. I was so flattered. Fiddle wanted to taste more of my cooking. So I said: come to South Africa! He did, but being a communist he kept swerving to the left and ended up in Angola!

Botha, P.W. The last Emperor of the 1000 bylaw Boer Reich. A bald, bland, unpleasant man with no sense of humour and an imperialist attitude to his position as a civil servant. I'd met him back in the early days, when he started out as the MP for George. Then he became various Deputy Ministers, always very full of himself and his destiny. In the regime of John Vorster, P.W. became Minister of Defence, a job I was earmarking for my husband Hasie! Imagine our disappointment! Botha prepared South Africa for a later war of his own making (see *War*). Soon we were marching into other people's countries and neighbourhoods, like Angola and Soweto. The 1978 Information Scandal (see *Information Scandal*) gave P.W. his chance to topple Vorster in a typical Broederbond coup (see *Vorster, John*). P.W. Botha became Prime Minister and later, through his new constitutional intrigues, Executive State President. If it wasn't for his wife Elize, there would've been no personal relationship with the First Couple for me. P.W. could not stand me and the feeling was mutual. But I loved Tannie Elize, a sweet kind woman who, as First Lady, would kick off her shoes and serve jellybabies to her guests. She kept her husband relatively sane. P.W. would have blown us all up, were it not for her. Eventually we had to get rid of him. Not easy but mercifully someone suggested putting Valiums in his orange juice. We did and F.W. de Klerk became his successor (see *F. W. De Klerk*). P.W. Botha is now in retirement in his home at the seaside outside, verily a voice in The Wilderness, just where he belongs. He refuses to take any responsibilities for the apartheid legacy and is still to consent to appear before the Truth and Reconciliation Commission (see *TRC*). He also has a new girlfriend!

Botha, Pik Roelof F. Botha: No relation to P.W. and the two couldn't have been further apart. The early Pik was vibrant and intense, a born actor and a great manipulator. His survival as the Talleyrand of Africa, the longest-serving Foreign Minister in the world, underlines this. I met him for the first time when he was our Ambassador to the UN (see *Bobotie*). What an attractive man: imagine him six foot tall (he still is, but mainly horizontal); pitch-black hair, shining with Brylcream or La Pebra, combed flat against his head as if licked by a mad cow. Those yellow lion eyes that could peer through your clothes into your deepest secrets. That sexy little moustache with a life of its own. Today it looks like a drowned mouse, but then the moustache gave him the look of the Errol Flynn of the National Party! Pik could give great speeches off the cuff. He had an unerring instinct for compromise when necessary. A great entertainer and host, a guru of wines, a great cook (see *Potjiekos*) and a best friend. Stories of our relationship beyond the call of duty are vicious and unnecessary. Pik was my boss as Minister of Foreign Affairs in charge of the Diplomatic

Corpse, when I was Ambassador (see *Bapetikosweti*). That's all. He even suggested ten years too early that we might have a black president. P.W. Botha nearly had a stroke. Or maybe he did, because his mouth sagged even more after that. President Mandela allowed Pik the Ministry for Minerals and Energy Affairs in the Government of National Unity. This was not a success. Pik never mixes minerals with anything! He is now semi-retired and writing his memoirs (see *Legal Action*).

Buthelezi, Mangosuthu Gatsha The Zulu that caused so much trouble! Our present Minister of Home Affairs, Buthelezi is a strange concoction of someone you're glad to see, while at the same time wishing he would go away! He takes himself very seriously, dressing up in various rare and protected skins while addressing his followers. I have seen leopard skins, cheetah skins, puma skins, zebra skins and, Pik swears, even a foreskin! He has a gift for making long rambling speeches inarticulately, usually with his eyes closed and his audience in a collective coma. He holds the record in that Guinness Book for making the longest Parliamentary speech in living memory! It went on for a few days with breaks for toilet and tea. Nelson Mandela, in his brilliance, knows it is better to keep Gatsha in the inner circle. While he and Thabo Mbeki were overseas recently, Mandela appointed Buthelezi as Acting President. We froze in horror. But it was a Sunday! No one was answering phones, so he couldn't declare KwaZulu-Natal independent, nor appoint Mandela as our new Ambassador to North Korea! And by the time Gatsha had stopped looking at the mirror, murmuring 'Viva President President President', it was Monday! And the real President was back! I strongly believe we should give Chief Buthelezi KwaZulu-Natal to play in and so get him out of our hair before he cuts off our heads!

Bapetikosweti The black homeland/Bantustan over which I reigned as South African Ambassador from 1984 to 1994. There were eight pieces of Bapetikosweti dotted all over white South Africa. We had a ninth little piece, but it was washed out to the sea during the 1986 floods. The President of Bapetikosweti was a sweet black man called Dr Professor Ignatius Makoeloeli. He was a friend of the family. We called him Pompies, because he was our garden boy for six years (see *Children*). My embassy had originally been my husband Hasie's family home, Liefdesbodem. In exchange for a few million rand, we allowed it to become the Embassy, 'BlancheNoir'. The border between South Africa and the homeland ran through our diningroom table. This all helped with later negotiations, as the ANC could sit in the homeland and the NP in South Africa and share the *Playboy* under the table! Nearby we had the Lunaville Hotel Complex, sister to Sun City in Bophuthatswana.

Biltong Delicious to eat, but difficult to explain. In fact, once explained, many people spit it out and vomit all over their nice jerseys. It is basically raw meat, hung out in the sun to dry. The fact that flies and maggots urinate, defecate, copulate, and then lay eggs in the meat while it hangs there, should be left out while explaining it to someone listening with a mouthful of biltong.

Boerewors Similarly with boerewors, or farmer's sausage to those who don't understand Afrikaans, although it sounds much worse in English! Delicious when barbecued. But what else is it other than a thin condom of ox-intestine stretched and filled with clumpy raw meat. Someone thought boerewors was related to haggis. Now that makes me want to vomit ...

Bafana Bafana South Africa's victorious football team that helped make us the proudest nation in the soccer world when they won the World Series in 1994. Since then they've had their ups and downs, but then, haven't we all?

Bloemfontein The capital of the Free State Province and the biggest city in the old Orange Free State. As nothing happens there, they know about everything else in the country. More or less the centre of South Africa. Relatively unspoilt and charming. Can be deadly boring on Sundays and hell in the heat.

Bad News I don't go for the negative (see *Good News*).

Books We used to read such a lot in the days when there was no television and when reading meant you could eventually have a conversation with someone else. It was the days when people could read. Not like today when most people can't. Then books cost less than going to the bioscope. Today you can buy a gun and use it for less than it will cost you to buy a book (see *AK47*). There is a huge problem here: if books cost more and more, and life is worth less and less, what message does this give us about the intention of our new government? Surely books should be subsidised, so that more people can discover the joy of using their imagination? The cheapest book around is Nelson Mandela's *Long Walk to Freedom*. If that can be sold cheaply, what about Jane Austen? Or the latest Jeffrey Archer?

Bioscope We were brought up in the bioscope. The Scala in Bethlehem, where we would spend so much time escaping from Real Life (see *Hollywood*). Today, going to the cinema is rare and usually a terrible strain. It's easier to watch a video. And cheaper. And your car doesn't get stolen.

Constitution We now have the most admired constitution in the world. It took an interim document and much midnight oil to sort it out. It was very important for us in the National Party to enshrine our minority rights in it, even though we had the irritation of being lumped together with lesbians, disabled people and mongoloids. But do we have a government strong and committed enough to protect this Constitution if and when challenged? This we will have to see. Will anyone keep an eye on the fragility of this perfection?

Communism Once the great evil, the bogeyman, the

devil, the enemy. The concept of share and share alike, that, like apartheid, could have worked if the sharing had been fair. But like apartheid, communism only benefited the ones who ruled, while the rest just shared their suffering! Someone wrote that if you are supportive of Communism as a youth, you are passionate; if you still support Communism in middle age, you are a fool! (See *ANC*) But now Communism is dead, like apartheid. The main enemy is gone. The armies of liberation are in a turmoil. The bleeding hearts are drowning in their old watery blood! There is no windmill left to confront! Shame! But South Africa, as true to form as always, is now the only country in the world with a Communist Party with plans for the future! The ANC is ruling in coalition with the SA Communist Party. Pretoria is full of Communists paying the rates and taxes. Hark! Do I hear Dr Verwoerd laughing in his grave? Or are the Communists laughing at me for thinking that they pay their rates and taxes?

Commonwealth The British Commonwealth comes to mind first. Happily, Dr Hendrik Verwoerd took us out of that in 1961, when we saw which way it was going: rowdy and black and very anti-Afrikaans! We were right. But as irony will have it, we are now back in the British Commonwealth! And now who is rowdy, black and very anti-Afrikaans? The New South Africa!

Colonialism The 17th Century must have been very boring, because everyone got onto small ships and seemed quite content to sail off the edge of the world, it being flat, as it was then. Some Spanish man sailed off and discovered America! Others from England found Australia. And of course our clever forefathers (see *Dutch*) found the Cape of Good Hope. Within a century the uncivilized world was colonized by the European nations. So there were those who were the natives, and those who were the overlords. Baas and Klaas. That's life. I'm just grateful we Europeans held the reins of power. But then the liberal bleeding hearts got coverage on television, and before you knew it, colonial ties were being cut, left, right and in Africa. All over the Dark Continent overnight and sometimes in the dead of night, some black terrorist was freed from jail, given a top hat and called President. Some minor Royal balding chinless wonder appeared from London to represent the British Crown. The Union Jack was quickly hauled down, bundled into a bag with some local priceless relics and everyone ran for the BOAC plane, leaving a new state to emerge choking from the chaos of civil war. Except in South Africa we got it right. Firstly we locked up all the big troublemakers and kept them in jail till they'd got their education. While they were studying on Robben Island, we Afrikaners, as Africans, held the power we took from the colonial overlord. In our case the cursed British Empire. We held democracy in trust till our black brothers and sisters were calm and adult enough to rule. And then we handed it to them, bit by bit. We still have a few bits in hand. No civil war, see?

Capitalism The other half of Communism and just as much a failure, except it could afford to survive. Seen by many as the accumulation of wealth, but like democracy less to it than meets the eye. Everyone dreams of being a capitalist, but it is easily sneered at by those who just can't seem to get their hands on the money. These anti-capitalists are often as greedy as those they attack, the terminal poor who have been instigated to rebellion by other greedy rich wanting it all for themselves. All under the pretext of sharing the spoils (see *Socialism*). None of it works. An eye for an eye and ten rand for one dollar, that's my motto!

Cape Town The Mother of all our Cities, our Womb with the view, a cradle of democracy. Still with the livid scar of District Six, her forced hysterectomy, still visible across her sagging abdomen. Will it still be known as Cape Town in the next century? Or will it be renamed 'Nelson's View', once poor old Johannesburg becomes SowetoWest and Durban Ulundi Ext 4?

Corruption Isn't it awful and a bit funny to see how our present ANC Government did not learn anything from the previous NP regime? It is now said: this government is more corrupt than the old one! Nonsense! No one could be more corrupt than the apartheid Broeders were! (Ask me; I was there. Not involved, mind you, just watching. Purely from the sidelines as a mere woman ...) No, this new lot are not more corrupt; just better at it!

Conscience I know that there are many stories going around about my supposed involvement with the apartheid state (see *TRC*), or my support of the former fascist structures of so-called white supremacist rule (see *Bapetikosweti*).

Whatever you have heard or read or think, I can assure you: my conscience is clear. Because I have never used it!

Condom A word I find difficulty in saying loudly in a public place. It seems though that it's time to grow up, because of the way things are developing! (See *AIDS*) My son De Kock encourages me to encourage you to use these condoms. Don't ask me why! Just do it. And I hope you're married to each other when you do!

Chauvinism We always used to call it Good Manners. Men opened doors for us, lit cigarettes for the ladies, paid the restaurant bills and generally behaved like gentlemen. That's also when ladies behaved like ladies. Now women behave like men, men dress up like women and the whole thing is a mess. A man's gentlemanly concern is now branded chauvinist by that shorthaired woman in pants with a hint of hair on her top lip and who still, ironically, expects to walk through a door first!

Coloureds An historical mistake made when white men without wives were forced into the servants' quarters to relieve themselves of a sort of biological need! No, let's be big about this: whites and blacks copulated and produced mixed-race babies. There, I've said it. Therefore the need for laws was obvious! (See *Immorality Act*) Today coloureds don't need blacks and whites to exist. They're very good at making themselves. And thanks to them, the National Party is still in power in the Western Cape!

Castro, Fiddle The leader-for-life of Cuba. One of the last of the Communist dinosaurs. And Pik tells me, he's been around for donkey's years. I remember meeting him in 1974 in New York (see *Botha, Pik*). Fiddle Castro was our first guest to taste my bobotie. He loved it. I was very scared of him. If you think Pik is tall at 6 foot? Castro is taller! And then, in those days he was younger and had very attractive eyes, before they went red and yellow. He wore a greenish, dirty uniform, and there were rows of medals. Real medals, hey? Not like the cardboard ones General Magnus Malan cut out of the Kelloggs Corn Flakes box! This Castro also had a big bushy beard. Poor old Fiddle. He came to Nelson Mandela's Inauguration and stole the show and, I think, some of the silver spoons. The First Lady of America, Mrs Clinton was terrified of meeting him. So we had to go back to some old apartheid tricks to keep them apart. Easily remembered, smoothly done.

Clinton, Bill Younger than me! Younger than most people I know. The most powerful man in the world, who has weak zippers and seems to spend a lot of time pulling up his trousers and then saying he never inhaled! When I see how easily he handles the TV cameras as if born with one in his face, I realise how we were handicapped. Remember how terribly badly our NP leaders came across on TV? I remember offering my services to P.W. as an experienced film actress. He turned me down. And look what happened to him! Clinton should get a Special Effects Oscar for his performance as President. His wife is even better at his job than he is.

Coertse, Mimi South Africa's prima opera diva and very good friend of mine. When Mimi went over to start her career at the Vienna State Opera in 1956, my sister Baby and I went along. It was our first visit to Europe. I hated Vienna, because no one spoke Afrikaans. But Mimi got us jobs in the chorus of the opera *Aida*! No sis, imagine, us having to play slave girls! Black slave girls! I refused to put on any of the black makeup. I was white, and white I was going to stay. So I was fired. Just typical communism!

Democracy Once too good to share with just anyone, democracy is now the most overused, most familiar, most misunderstood concept in the land.

No one is ever happy in a democracy, so South Africa's probably a healthy one. If someone is happy, there's something wrong with the democracy. The happiness of one citizen too often means the suffering of another. I like this democracy as long as I don't have to vote for someone I can't control.

Diplomacy Pik taught me: diplomacy is the art of getting on with those whom you cannot stand. And I've been doing it for years with great success.

DP The Democratic Party is filling its necessary job as the fox terrier round the feet of the lumbering ANC rhino. Led by a young Tony Leon, the DP has constantly kicked the laurels out from under itself and called on the status quo to explain itself. The DP has always managed to straddle the extremes of local politics without getting its equipment wet.

Where would we in the NP be without them? In the dark days of apartheid, it was the courage and the guts of the PFP led by Helen Suzman (see *Suzman*) that exposed the old NP pigs wallowing in the stench of their corruption. Then thanks to DP policy, F.W de Klerk saw their blueprint for survival and saw the light (see *De Klerk*). He hijacked the DP platform and so won half of a Nobel Peace Prize. In the process he lost a country. The DP has proved itself a strong and committed supporter of democratic principles, at the expense of being called racists by the blacks caught with their fat fingers in the national cookie jar.

De Klerk, F.W. The white knight in shining armour that scooped South Africa out of the quicksand of legalised racism and delivered us in one piece at the feet of the black messiah? Not so simple! When we got P.W. out of his office (see *Botha, P.W.*) Pik and I had to find a new leader. The choices in the National Party caucus were dire. It was then that I espied a bald head bobbing outside the double doors. It was F.W. de Klerk having a quick smoke behind the proteas. (He tends to smoke like a guilty schoolboy, surreptitiously behind his hand.) I suddenly realised that he looked just like P.W. Botha! Same bald head, same glasses, same problem. No one would know the difference! We wouldn't have to change the stamps and the coins. I pointed him out to Pik. But Pik wanted to be the next President, but I said: 'No man, I need you with me! Finish en klaar!' So I called F.W. He came over. 'Hello Tannie Evita?' I said: 'Put out that cigarette!' He did on the carpet! I said: 'F.W.? Do you know how to spell the word Democracy?' He said: 'No.' I said:

'You're the next President of South Africa!' But, gosh, was I wrong? Look what he did. F.W. took us out of the darkness into the light! (See *Thatcher*) Sadly F.W. didn't listen to his immaculate sense of timing. He should have left the political stage in 1996, once the National Party left the Government of National Unity, and dumped the carcass of the NP in someone else's lap. History would have remembered him as the White Knight. Instead De Klerk stayed behind, trying to recreate an ex-party out of an ex-pariah. Maybe his wife Marike didn't want to leave the portals of power. He read the Xhosa writing on the wall and resigned as NP leader in August 1997, leaving a party in crisis and me wondering if this is my next move? Evita – successor to De Klerk?

De Lille, Patricia A leading light in the PAC (See *PAC*) But one of the few alternative politicians that make me wonder what she's doing wasting her time in the PAC with a lot of marginalised out-of-date Marxist losers. We could use her in the centre of policymaking and government. I like her, in spite of the fact that I should run fast when I see her.

Droëwors A relation to boerewors and biltong, except it's also dried and delicious and never to be analysed. Mad Cow Disease is a picnic in comparison to what lurks there!

English Among the eleven official languages, English is the favoured unofficial first language of this new South Africa. Sadly the good old days of the Queen's English is went! No small thanks to the hatchet job done to the tongue by the SABC, which in the unseemly rush towards affirmative action (see *Affirmative Action*) seems to hand the live microphone to any black twirp with an Afro hairdo and a speech defect. They then proceed to assassinate the vowel sounds within seconds of clearing their throats. Or were those supposed to be the consonants? As American is the language of the computer, and of Hollywood, and because it is vaguely related to English, the language of Shakespeare and the Beatles has a slight hope of survival.

Election The Thesaurus adds the following alternatives: 'appointment, choice, preference, selection'. Nowhere does the word 'fun' appear, which is a great shame. Because the enjoyment of having an election is surely the excitement of voting someone out and choosing someone else to take over.

Our elections in the past were so simple. Firstly, there was no need to really fight elections, as the NP Government always won every election. Opposition was locked up and couldn't vote. Not because they were in jail; but because they weren't white! It was also easy to encourage the support of your local candidate after his election. You started off by bringing him melktert and koeksisters, buying him a new car and treating him to a nice holiday in Mauritius. Then you made sure that everyone voted for him, even at great personal expense. Call it investment, or just write it off against tastes. You knew, that when his official phone rang in his office in Parliament and he heard it was you, he was that mere servant who owed you a favour! No longer, alas!

We now vote only for a party. 'Proportional Representation' has cut out the human contact. Oh shame, if only there was still fun attached to an election? Why not just say: 'Come and have a party!' Believe me, there's really nothing that a good party can't cure. So you'd better find one before the 1999 Election! (Otherwise call me and I'll suggest one!)

Emigration & Exile Whereas daily one is aware of the many citizens of our fair land who pulled up their tent pegs, pressed diamonds into the wet biltong and escaped to the fairer fields of Australia and America, it is heartwarming to notice so many former fleeees returning home after decades abroad. For them to fit into the new South Africa again after all these years is often like trying to force a square peg into a round hole. When going into either self-imposed or forced exile, the inner timeclock too often stops dead at that last moment of memory. Many of our returning South Africans are bewildered when they don't or can't recognise the same country they left behind in the '60s, the '70s or the '80s. The tepid, polluted and exhausted sunsets in Clifton will never be the same as those familiar warm and golden ones on the old SAA posters left behind on so many kitchen doors in foreign lands.

Education So much to teach; so little time; so few teachers; so much red tape; so little money; so many blueprints; so little care; such bad speling … sppelish … spellingh … ag nee, man …

Europe The pod from which many of our seeds sprang;

the ancient root of our evils; the eurocentric breath in our top *c*'s; the *thou* in our crippled speech; the yellowed and nearly forgotten link with an old world long gone and so far far away.

Evita Peron Some blonde third-rate actress in a South American country, who married a weak but ruthless politician, made him famous and beloved of his people, wore pretty clothes and jewels that they paid for and then died of cancer in her early thirties. *Belaglike storie!* No relation or connection to me whatsoever: 1. I do not have a musical written about me. 2. I don't sing everything and 3. I am still alive! As for my real name: it's Evangelie Poggenpoel. So don't cry for me.

Enemies They are always the obvious ones. The jealous ones, the stupider ones, the losers, the fakers, the pretenders. Like a bad smell, you know how to avoid them. It is the friends that turn against you in secret behind their loving hugs that are the most dangerous. The ones who condemn you with a smile and sell you out with a kiss. The old adage that your enemy's enemy is your friend is a constant in politics. And in South Africa more than anywhere else, we have realised how flimsy the substance of The Enemy is (see *Propaganda*). We confronted our enemy in terror and then realised that there was little difference between us. We all laughed at the same jokes! An enemy is often just a convenience. A bad friend is always a terrible problem and a real loss.

Environment If you've planted a tree that will only be at its best years after you've died, you'll understand Environment. If you chop down trees because they're in the way, you won't know what we're talking about (see *Stupid*).

Family Unfortunately a family is not something you can choose, like a friend or a pet. You're stuck with them, come hell or high water. And with mine I've been through both. My own family from my mother's side (see *Mother*) is small and I am familiar with them: Ma, Baby my sister, and me. Then as for punishment I married into the Bezuidenhout family: Hasie, my husband, and his three sisters and their horrible husbands and hatreds and intrigues. Napoleon would understand. Family usually always comes first, even though they don't last. Family is either a joy from beginning to end, or just a heavy burden that slows you down as you hurtle down the precipice of ambition. You choose!

Fascism What is this horrible word that sounds so wrong and feels so familiar? Is fascism the belief that you are better than others? That your tribe deserves a front pew in the church? That those with funny faces must be asked to leave society? I've seen films about Hitler and Mussolini. The actor who played the Italian Fascist wasn't good, so I'm not convinced that Mussolini was all bad. But were we Afrikaners like them? Was apartheid fascist? Or simply just wrong. Or right, but at the wrong time in history? Or what? Maybe it is just one of those damn isms that haunt us. This is obviously political. Out of the mouths of liberals, fascism sounds like a devil's disease. Out of the mouths of conservatives it sounds like an old recurring allergy. And out of the mouths of many of my contemporaries, fascism just sounds like the English word for Afrikaner Nationalism.

Food You are what you eat.

Fashion You can be a slave to fashion. But once you realise who decides what fashion is, you realise that fashion is what you create around what makes you look good. I have worn darkdark sunglasses in winter and created fashion. I have worn hats that become the rage. I have dressed in what I like with pride and confidence. Knowing that no woman would wear the same. Originality! For the simple reason that my maid ran it up on her Singer in her room the night before. I have been well dressed by some of our great fashion emperors. Chris Levin has always been my favourite, because of his sense of humour. Sometimes I would try on something just because I felt like it. He would stand back and laugh at me! *Die kabouter!* I then knew not to buy it! When he frowned and used more than ten pins, I ordered four of each. And when he just closed his eyes and said: 'Darlingkie...' I knew I had hit the jackpot.

Flags After decades of living under the flapping, silly concoction of orange, white and blue, held together by three small flags in the centre like pieces of elastoplast, we have an original flag that represents the New South Africa. It has Red, Blue, Green, Black and Gold in it somewhere. It looks a bit like part of a giant's Y-fronts. But everyone seems satisfied. I don't want to take credit, but it took locking

Roelf Meyer and Cyril Ramaphosa in our spare room for a weekend with a box of crayons, a bottle of Cream Soda and a packet of NikNaks for them to come up with this final design. They did!

Foreigners Too many of them around to feel comfortable about them. Call them tourists, illegal immigrants, new wives, third husbands, visitors, businessmen, interested parties, whatever. Unless they live down the road and you know them from school, don't talk to them. Go home, hide the silver and lock the door!

Fun Having fun in South Africa is becoming one of the rarest of pastimes. In the old days you could get into your car with a picnic basket and drive for one hour, stop, walk into the veld and have fun. Nowadays you get hijacked at the first robot! There is no open veld between here and forever! It's too dangerous walking in the veld anyway. You'll be raped by a criminal out on bail for rape and probably murdered. And they won't even bother to steal the picnic basket because they're vegetarians! Fun today is sitting at home behind a locked door praying no one will find you.

Felicia Mabusa-Suttle A returned exile of light-brown hue, who never stops telling us on public television how she was once a simple black girl from the dusty streets of Soweto, who went to America and got married and came back as South Africa's answer to Oprah Winfrey. Our answer to that? Our question probably is: who thinks she is a talk-show hostess and isn't? Our Felicia! *Foeitog!* She also had a stint as PR for SAA. Having painted the Olympics Boeing singlehanded with her nail polish (no wonder it looks such a mess; Felicia will never wear her glasses in public!), all the airhostesses also started to look like her! Most alarming, especially the men! Her TV show sounds like an argument in the street and looks like something that happens while people are waiting for a powercut to end. I wish her on no one I like (see *Death Penalty*).

Faxing I can't imagine what we did without the fax machine. Then it took time to communicate; one also had time to reconsider! Now it just takes the pressing of a button! How many faxes I sent and regretted in the morning? I've stopped talking about faxing in Afrikaans, because the word has invited strange reactions from stupid people. When I was asked on television if I'd seen Pik Botha recently, I answered in Afrikaans: 'He faxes me every night' (*Hy faks my elke aand.*) He does. But in English!

Folksongs 'Sarie Marais!' 'Daar kom die Alabama!' 'Hoe lê die wêreld tog so blou!' 'Jan Pierewiet!'.... Hundreds of wonderful tunes that we as Afrikaans children sang constantly. At school, at picnics, in the bus, at the braaivleis. A great bible of folksongs is the *FAK Sangbundel*. It chills the soul ever so slightly when one realises, as I didn't, that many of our favourite harmless songs were taken over from the marching anthems of the Nazi soldiers and just translated into Afrikaans. Of course, it was my sister who exploded the myth of originality in our culture (see *Sister*). I still get a lump in my throat when I hear 'Sarie Marais' sung, especially when I'm far away from home, in the Kremlin or the White House.

God Someone I was very scared of for most of my life. More threatening than a Commission of Inquiry or journalist. In my tortured mind, God tended to look a lot like an old Charlton Heston as Moses. Then He started looking like an angry Dutch Reformed elder. Then He looked like Hendrik Verwoerd! When Verwoerd was killed, the image of God also disappeared. Although it's tempting to put God out of your mind after watching the TV news about what's happening in Rwanda, or in Cambodia, or in a terminal cancer ward, I need the need of a God more than the satisfaction of logic. I still believe deep down that it's a sin to even discuss God, so I'll stop (see *Dutch Reformed Church*).

Great Trek The forced migration of hundreds of peace-loving Christian Boer citizens who couldn't stand another moment living under the oppressive yoke of British Imperialism. That's a pretty good definition that would have given me a gold star at school. It was a magnificent moment in our history: women and children, men and youths, combining their passion for liberty and carrying their fat oxen and heavy wagons across the vast and vicious Drakensberg. That's true: my forefathers did that! Imagine carrying your Toyota over a mountain? Impossible without help? So you know! My new friends in the ANC now assure me that the Voortrekkers were actually on the run from the Colonial Police for stealing cattle and raping black women. Someone else will have to believe today's history books, ink still wet.

But the Great Trek is a symptom of a collective malaise: Afrikaners cannot stick together. There is nothing worse for an Afrikaner than being with another Afrikaner. So we Afrikaners have been trekking since the beginning of our history. Either from one side of the country to the other, from one side of the town to another. Or in this world, sometimes from the ground floor to the 45th. The Great Trek continues. Often within.

Gold All that glitters is not gold, they say? Often they lie. Gold has been the foundation of so many Afrikaner dreams. It was in our ground for us to remove, a special gift from God. The world wanted our gold, so we thought it would never allow us to go black. The price of gold was not interested in human fights, just ownership rights. Just some of the nonsense we believed for all those years of isolation. Gold is drying up. The world has enough in vaults and safes. The price is still falling. What more can I tell you? I have some old gold rings for sale! Any decent offers?

Grandchildren I have five! My pride and joy. Billie-Jeanne married Leroy Makoeloeli in 1990. It was a scandal. Evita's daughter marries a black! I nearly died, but mercifully Leroy is nearly white in his education and manners. I sometimes prefer him to my own son Izan. Their first child, named after its mother and the Mother of the Nation, is Winnie-Jeanne. Very artistic, especially in doing tricks with matches and tyres. Then comes the little boy, Nelson-Ignatius. And the smallest one is little La Toya-Ossewania. She is teaching me how to dance the toyi-toyi, and I show her how to do *volkspele*. They have made me feel so ashamed about my terrible prejudices of the past. How could we blame children for colour? They are innocent and colourless until they start stealing. Then they become black! The only problem is, I can't see them in the dark! So now when I go into their playroom, I knock at the door and say: 'Smile, here comes Gogo!' And then they all smile and thank heavens I can see their little white teeth and not fall over them and break their arms and legs. Izan and his Annabella have given me two blond blue-eyed grandsons. They have no sense of humour and frighten me to death!

Gossip The difference between gossip and rumour is that one is not true and the other is false. After all these years of instigating both, I still cannot tell the difference!

Gardens I love my gardens and have a very close relationship with whoever works in them. My fingers aren't green enough to make the garden grow by itself. Need black fingers to do that. Some of my best friends have worked in my garden: Nelson Mandela pruned roses while convalescing in secret from TB, while still a banned non-person. And my daughter Billie-Jeanne's father-in-law, Ignatius Makoeloeli, was our garden boy for six years. Before he became President of Bapetikosweti.

Gay Liberation I think all liberation movements have been far too serious for far too long. They must be more happy; lighter and also friendlier. So the day the ANC and the AWB go gay, will be a happy day for South Africa. My

The proud grandmother-of-the-nation with little Winnie-Jeanne Makoeloeli

son De Kock just laughs till he cries when I say this. I wished he wouldn't do that in public. His medicinal black-eye make-up runs, which he has to wear against allergies. The doctor gave him a certificate to support that. Now, why am I telling you all this …

Ginwala, Frene The present Speaker of Parliament. Dr Ginwala some years ago invited me to join the ANC Women's League. She said: 'Stop being Pik's puppet and stand up for your rights!' I was tempted. Pik was very sarcastic and wanted to tie my arms with rope to the window bars, but I said: 'Ag nee, Pik, what if your secretary comes in …' Dr Ginwala is a very good Speaker, although she talks too much. Her deeds are more tangible than her words. She has managed to clean up the whole of Parliament and get rid of all the mementoes of the past. All the paintings and sculptures of the old South Africa have been removed. They have been replaced by obscene images in an exhibition of anti-apartheid art. If that's what the world gets without apartheid, think again! No South African artists are represented; just nasty amateur political graffiti merchants. My worst is the one with Mandela on the cross and Vorster as the soldier pressing a spear into his side! Sies, Frene, sies! (See *Parliament*)

Gravy Train As far as I am concerned, I can say: the Gravy Train does not stop here any more!

Hope Hope springs eternal? That can be seen as weakness, or as a result of too much to drink! I've always had hope, for the simple reason that without it there was no hope. So I keep hoping.

Hypocrisy I saw it written with lipstick on a mirror in the ladies' toilet of 10 Downing Street while Maggie was in residence: 'Hypocrisy is the Vaseline of Political Intercourse'! I'm still not sure what it means, but people always applaud when I say it during speeches and say how satirically pertinent a comment it is! Goodness me!

Homosexual There are lots of them overseas, I am told. Homosexuality is a contagious sexual diversity among American, English, German and French youths. Also coloureds, but what can you expect from such inbreeding. Definitely not Afrikaners. I've never heard of an Afrikaner who is one. No, wait…eh…no, that strange Ashley Vermeulen boy was really Jewish and only spoke Afrikaans to be friendly. I wished my son De Kock wouldn't be so sociable. Always wants to help those who need it. And he is not shy to invite some of these afflicted boys over to spend the weekend! I keep warning him about homosexuals. But then Pik explained to me that Man started as a *homo sapiens*, then grew to a *homo erectus*. So blow me down, if this *homo sexual* isn't becoming more normal by the day!

History I suppose History is Everyman's vision of yesterday. Someone somewhere always seems to decide what is History and what is nonsense. History always turns the other cheek when she smiles at the winner. Losers get the bad publicity (see *Nazis*); winners don't. The losers of wars always had the 'worst massacres' and 'biggest concentration camps'. And of course killed 'millions upon millions'! The winners of wars always 'liberated the oppressed', 'saved democracy' and then 'reestablished world order'! But each side had the same weapons and the same hatred and as much to lose! There is a special department in Pretoria that rewrites South Africa's history. What was historically accepted ten years ago has been politically rearranged for today. Example: 1985 – 'Jan van Riebeeck landed in the Cape in 1652, and brought civilization to darkest Africa.' 1996 – 'Jan van Riebeeck was an escaped Dutch convict who raped black women on Robben Island'! It is said that history never repeats itself; it just takes tragedy and turns it into farce (see *New South Africa*). Often it doesn't have to repeat itself, it only rhymes! (See *Bosnia*)

Honesty Is it the best policy? Not if your policy depends on dishonesty (see *Apartheid, Thatcherism, Democracy*, etc.).

Holiday Never something I could enjoy. Throughout my husband's career, his holiday meant the time I worked the hardest. Entertaining his friends, fixing his clothes, keeping the children out of his way. Their holiday meant I worked harder than ever fixing their clothes and keeping them out of their father's way. And my only holiday was when I missed a plane in Johannesburg and could spend a night at the Holiday Inn! What a holiday that was!

Heritage It's all we have to remember us by!

Hangover Here is Pik's wonderful treatment for a hangover: another drink! Or a Bloody Winnie, which is like a Bloody Mary but drunk out of a rubber cup! Or just drink lots of water the night before you go to bed. Or just stop drinking!

Holomisa, Bantu Formerly a General in the Transkei Army who took control of that homeland in a coup. We always suspected he was just harbouring the ANC and he proved us right. He immediately slid into the upper echelon of the ANC and became a Deputy Minister in the GNU. Rumours of his volatile relationship with radical elements in the ANC (see *Winnie*) and his recent shocking disclosure of corruption in government to the Truth Commission (see *Corruption*) led to his dismissal and final banishment from the party. Holomisa proves that there is freedom of speech in the ANC: it is after speech that freedom goes. He is now a potential leader in search of a new party. Typical of a man like Holomisa to have the name Bantu. Just call him by name and people say you're a racist! I asked him once: 'Do you have a real name?' He said: 'Johannes Petrus!' I said: 'No man, stick to Bantu!'

International In a modern world everything fashionable is international: Hillbrow, London, New York, Hong Kong, Los Angeles and even Amsterdam. The foyer of all the Hilton Hotels, Holiday Inns, Sheratons and Hyatts are international. So is CNN. American culture is now international, as it has been forced down all our throats under the guise of freedom of expression! Just look at the United States of

America! International at birth; made up of immigrants from all over the world. Marriages between black and white are now international. Business is; money should be. The World! All international. So what is all this nonsense about retaining a national identity? There is no such thing.

Intimidation The worst type of democratic way to get someone to do things your way. It happens daily in all areas of life. At election time, intimidation is in full swing. Tip: when there is a knock at the front door during the election campaign and you open the door to reveal your worst nightmare come true, say what they want to hear: 'Yes, I'll vote for you! Viva! Amandla! Vrystaat! Ole!' Etc.! Say anything to stay alive and keep your house in one piece. Because voting is secret! No one will know who you voted for.

Image A concept that is becoming more important than the object itself. Image is all. Encased in hype and carried along by merchandise and PR, image will soon rule the world. TV is all image. Adjectives are image. Politics is image. People have become the wrappings of image. I hate it. I hope I don't ever need it.

Indira Ghandi She ruled India as Prime Minister till she was shot by her own security guards! And I will not take any blame here. Yes, it is true she was eating bobotie she had made from my own recipe. Yes, it is true that she went to say goodbye to her guests at the gate. Yes, it is true she was supposed to go to her office. Yes, it is true that she decided to slip back into the dining-room for another plate of my bobotie. Yes, it is true that she was shot on her way to my bobotie! And no, it is not true that I can be blamed for her death!

Internet The modern spider's web which, thank God, I am now too old-fashioned to understand. But I am told by my son De Kock that even I have a Webpage on the Internet: so see you there! http://www.millennia.co.za/evita.

Individual Just you or just me. Never mind the other billions of people. Take away me, and that leaves you. Individual means only one of a kind. And only one person in the universe. The only view of the world. In fact: the only view. The rest is rumour and propaganda. Once the individual becomes the people, there is no view of the world. Just policy. Just us and them. Never again you and me. And sadly no longer just I!

Immorality The word can only be associated with that terrible mistake we made: the Immorality Act. In order to stop our people from sexually crossing the colour bar, we turned it into a crime. Instead of just letting them get on with it and realising what a burden it placed on the children that followed, we invited the wrath of the world, who condemned the law for its inhumanity. And out of jealousy that they didn't think of it first! Ironic note: today I am here as a relation of someone who broke that law! My own daughter has a black husband! See? I said it out loud and nothing has changed. He's still black, she's still my daughter and you're no longer shocked.

Immigrants In many societies immigrants were the ones who did all the hardest work for the least reward except for just being a citizen of a new land; that was the greatest prize. South Africa is also a land of immigrants. We Afrikaners came as Dutch, and mingled with the British, Germans, French, etc. The blacks came down from the Sahara and we met up somewhere near the Fish River (see *Great Trek*). And today we are a totally colourblind society. But immigration does not stop with a word. Since the end of Influx Control (see *Apartheid*) we are now hosting up to 5 million illegal immigrants, mainly from the rest of Africa. Nigerians seem to come hand in glove with the drug trade. Seeing so many new black faces in the streets, I now realise that not all blacks look alike. Just our Xhosa and Zulu.

Instinct Something I have learnt not to ignore. I seldom understand it, but follow it without question. It has made me the most famous white woman in South Africa and unquestionably one of the three most famous and admired Afrikaners in the world.

Irrelevant Probably the most frightening word to end up becoming. But once it happens there is something very liberating in admitting: I am a member of an irrelevant white minority. That means that whatever you do will have no political influence on the way the country is going. And therefore no political blame. It also means that whatever you do can now be of your choice and not as a result of expectation. I am irrelevant; therefore I am!

Jewellery I love jewellery! I used to have a wonderful collection, but when P.W. Botha left power, we realised our collecting days were numbered. So most of the jewels were handed back to a man called Herman in Pik's department and...? Well, I'm not sure where they are. Pik says there's nothing to worry about, but I do worry. I have some nice costume jewellery pieces De Kock brought me from New York. No one knows the difference! In fact, a mugger once pulled my necklace off in the women's toilet of the Stock Exchange in Johannesburg. When I recognised her and went to her house the next day, I gave her R20 in exchange for the necklace. She was very grateful. Haai shame, she'd lost her job to an affirmative tea girl. What she wanted with my paste necklace is a mystery. I only wear jewellery when I'm on duty. I want the people to see me at my best and realise that although they all look and feel drab, at least one of us is still looking wonderful, wealthy and white.

Journalists Never been my favourite animal. Always seem to be holier than thou, and filled with a crusader's zeal to find the truth, the whole truth and nothing but the truth. But who often give up, because it's too difficult to find the real truth. So they just publish whatever they can suck out of their thumbs. Or whoever's thumb is in reach! Journalism is an art form that has certainly lost its practitioners in South Africa (see *Media*).

Jackson, Jesse He is the only member of the Jackson Family who doesn't look like Diana Ross. An American politician who seems to need South African politics to get him publicity at home. It seems whenever we were releasing blacks from jail, Jackson's face could be seen in a corner of the photo. I think he is one of those frantic liberals who will never forgive fate for not having had them assassinated and so made immortal.

Ja-Nee The most charming explanation of the essence of being an Afrikaner. It simply means: YesNo.

Kaffir And here it is! No sis! This was a horrible word that some people have used for too long and too often. It degrades and embarrasses black people and that's something I never want to do. But gosh, it's hard in the traffic! When those damn taxis cut in front of you and nearly drive you off the road? And you can't help but shout: "Donnerse Kaffir!"? I shouldn't: I'm working at it, but old habits die hard.

Kultuur Nothing to do with Culture, although it's the Afrikaans word for it. *Kultuur* became the cement with which various parts of the Boer Empire were glued together. It was important to live up to the expectations we inherited from the Germans and their 'Kultur'. We also wanted writers like Goethe, Schiller and that other one I can never remember. Where were our great musical geniuses like Wagner and Beethoven? Even a filmmaker like Leni Riefenstahl, even though she got found out to be a Nazi. So we encouraged Ons Kultuur. Anyone who underlined our policy with poetry or plays, those we rewarded with prizes and good reviews. South Africa was soon awash with

Afrikaans novelists, Afrikaans poets, Afrikaans dramatists, Afrikaans painters, Afrikaans sculptors and even one Afrikaans satirist, although he didn't have much talent or last long. These pocketbook Kultuurists embellished the Afrikaner Dream with the substance of 'Kultur'. It separated us from the killers and thugs that we must have been, and turned us into a nation of artists and persons of culture. It didn't work. Apartheid is dead, and so is the majority of our Kultuur. At least the Nazis had Leni Riefenstahl. We had nothing!

Koornhof, Dr Piet Once the second most powerful politician in P.W. Botha's government. At various times he was Minister of Sport, then Education, Plural Development and other fancy things, before becoming our Ambassador in the USA. A delightful man with huge ears and a long nose; looks like reject from the Disney Shop. He has a sense of humour that belies a sharp sense of survival. I remember him saying: 'When I make a law, it soon becomes a joke; when I make a joke, it becomes a law!' Piet is the one Afrikaner who proved to the world that we can adapt. Once he retired at the end of the 1980s, he met a nice young woman of colour (see *Coloureds*). They now live together happily and visibly. She has a child, maybe by him, and had twins this year. I asked Piet: 'Piet, are you the father of the twins?' He just said: 'Ja-nee!'

Killarney Studios Where I made my films in the 1950s. I won a competition in a local Afrikaans magazine and went to Killarney Studios for a film test. The director was Pierre de Wet. I passed the test. I made 'Boggel en die Akkedis', 'Meisie van my Drome' and 'Duiwelsvallei'. My last film was never finished. It was too political. Hendrik Verwoerd stopped it. Rather than blame him, I became his friend (see *Verwoerd*). My husband soon became a minister. The rest is history. A better investment than a fading acting career in Afrikaans films!

Koeksisters A wonderful sticky, messy, delicious thing that defies any description. We have it for tea, with coffee, or just when the need for sugar overpowers the need for image. My recipe for Koeksisters is also world-famous and here it is:

Evita Bezuidenhout's World-famous Recipe for Koeksisters

Syrup	Batter
100 ml sugar	500 ml flour
500 ml water	10 ml baking powder
5 ml vanilla essence or	5 ml salt
grated orange rind or	70 ml margarine
cinnamon or	1 egg
1,5 ml ginger	80 ml milk
5 ml cream of tartar	oil for frying
2,5 ml tartaric acid	

Method
To make syrup, boil sugar, water, flavouring, cream of tartar and tartaric acid until syrupy, about 10 minutes. Set aside to cool.
To make batter, sift dry ingredients. Cut or rub margarine into dry ingredients lightly. Beat egg well and mix with milk. Add egg and milk to flour mixture, handling as little as possible. Leave in refrig-

erator for at least 1 hour. Roll out dough to thickness of 0,4 cm. Cut into strips, 8 cm in length and 2,5 cm in width. Cut each strip into 2 or 3 lengthwise, leaving one side uncut. Twist or plait loose pieces around one another and press ends together firmly. Deep fry in hot oil until golden brown. Dip hot koeksisters into cool syrup, drain and cool. Koeksisters can be stored in refrigerator for up to 1 week.

Karoo The jewel in the crown of thorns that is our heritage. A barren wasteland of koppies and dried riverbeds, of knobbly trees and antheaps. Dry in summer, but within hours of rain, a flower show. Sunsets are unique and sunrises poetic. The Karoo stretches from the Hex River Mountains in the south to the Orange River in the north. And yet, flying over it, one doesn't realise that it all basically belongs to six farmers who voted Nat in 1948.

Kennedy Family The American Bezuidenhouts.

Love If all is for love, then the pain was worthwhile. If not, I wish someone had warned me in time.

Language My first language has always been Afrikaans. Then out of necessity we had to learn English, as both were our official languages. But now suddenly we have to have eleven official languages! English, Afrikaans, Zulu, Xhosa, North Sotho, South Sotho, Venda, Shangaan, Swati, Pedi....? And what's the eleventh? Kugel? Cape Coloured? Not very practical. I mean, what happens if you have a vicious rottweiler at home? What language do you put on the sign? Or do you use all eleven languages? Does the sign become the gate? Imagine, eleven times: Beware of the Dog, Oppas vir die Hond, Umkhonto weSizwe, and on and on and on! By the time your Venda guest has been looking for his language, the dog has already bitten him on his backside! The best suggestion is to learn one sentence in all eleven languages: 'I am on your side!' But never say it in Xhosa to a Zulu! (See *Zulu*)

Life The older I get the more I enjoy Life, but it's going by quicker and quicker each year. I now can look back on a longer life behind me than ahead of me. But it's the only one I've been given, so I will make the best of it while I still have it.

Libra My birth sign. I was born on 28th September 1935, which makes me a Libran. Traditionally we can't make up our minds and when we do, we want to change our decisions. This is probably true with normal Librans. I am exceptional, because I have traits associated with Virgo, Taurus, Leo and Scorpio. Libra is probably what I am when I sleep.

Liberals Those who bend over blackwards!

Marriage Call me old-fashioned, but marriage is something I support fully. I do not agree with this modern contempt for the legality of a union between man and woman. There is a good reason for it, so there's no reason to ignore it. I've been lucky, married to Hasie for all these years. It was give and take. Not always what you expect. If you think a marriage will develop in one way, it evolves in another. Marriage is full of surprises, the biggest one being suddenly aware that you have been married for over 40 years! And when you close your eyes, you can't remember what he looks like!

Minority Rights This could frankly mean anything. Everyone is part of some or other minority: shortsighted people, those with crinkly red hair, those with webbed feet, those with freckles. The list of exceptions to the rule is endless. If the answer is that everyone has rights, the question is why? To think that you are born with all the rights is a bit cheeky. Fighting for rights makes sense. Losing rights through carelessness is a good lesson. As a white Afrikaner Calvinist I have always enjoyed minority rights over a majority! Nice, hey? But I think we were the last ones to get away with that.

Machel, Graça The elegant widow of former Mozambique President Samora Machel. He was suddenly killed when his plane thought a hill in the Kruger National Park was an airport. Pik swears we had nothing to do with it. Graça is now Nelson Mandela's latest girlfriend. What a treat to see them together! They hold hands like schoolkids! Oh please, let that dear old man find happiness, and someone at home when he comes back from work who is (a) not breaking in to steal the TV; (b) not creeping out after a session with Winnie or (c) not a German banker waiting for a long boring meeting about investment. Let Nelson come home to a wife who will love him and hold him! Also politically, Nelson must get married! And Graça is so perfect: gracious, bright, a leader in her own right. So when he 'moves on', he will leave behind a Widow Mandela, and not just a half-deranged ex-Mrs Mandela!

Malan, D.F. The first Afrikaner NP Prime Minister to take office in 1948. He was a NGK dominee too, but I fear he had no luck with his hot line to heaven. Or whoever answered the phone from up there only spoke Xhosa! He was before my time; I only knew him as an airport.

Mbeki, Thabo Present Deputy President and Heir Apparent. If this happens, our dreams will be fulfilled. He is a charming man who studied where Shakespeare and Mozart were not regarded as Eurocentric upstarts. He understands delicate First World sensitivities, but can also sink to the lowest common denominator and toyi-toyi till the cows come home. He works all the time, has managed to clear the field of all his opponents (see *Ramaphosa*), but his close relationship to Winnie is worrying. To us whites. Which is irrelevant, isn't it?

Melktert Milk tart? Sounds so feeble in English, like so many forced translations of Afrikaans passions. I make a *wonderful* melktert.

Medical We used to have one of the best medical professions in the world. I only have to mention Dr Christiaan Barnard and his heart transplants. But since Dr Zuma has become Minister of Health (see *Zuma*), we have lost faith in our talents to heal. Most of our white doctors have emigrated to Australia and the USA. It makes me angry to know that they were happy to stay on in South Africa and benefit from our white apartheid education, while now being the first to bleat their hatred of that bad system, while making money in other civilized countries. So now in order to heal our blacks, we're stuck with 250 Cuban doctors! What do they know? All they've brought us is Castroenteritis! Now in SA, when you feel a cold coming on, take a plane and go sneeze in Canada!

Meyer, Roelf Once the leading light of the NP, who with Cyril Ramaphosa helped formulate the new Constitution and design the flag (see *Flag*). A bright young man who still calls me Tannie, he was recently forced out of the NP by what Pik calls 'a menopausal twitch' from FW's sunset reign as NP leader. Roelfie has the trust of the people. What will happen to him now? A new party with Bantu?

Mother Ossewania Kakebenia Poggenpoel, my mother, was born on 1st January 1900 in the Heldersonop Concentration Camp outside Bloemfontein. She has never forgiven the English for the Boer War! She is still alive, living in an old-age home with a young one-legged surfer, whom she is teaching how to do the macarena! What can I say about my mother? A man's mind, a staunch Nationalist, a Calvinist, a Christian, a moral pillar of society. She brought us up with the will to live and the need to fight. 'Never lie down and let them walk over you,' she said, and we didn't. And if we had to lie down, they lay down with us! I don't know who my father was, but if my dear mother liked him enough to give him koffie and beskuit, then that's alright by me. We don't get on very well, because I keep wishing she'd start forgetting those things best left forgotten! But even at 97 years old, she remembers every damn detail. Of everything! I tell everyone she's mad, but I know she's not.

Mandela, Nelson After 27 years of hell, this remarkable ex-terrorist, ex-convict, most-feared enemy-of-my-state, comes into my life and forgives me! Me! Afrikaner Nationalist! I once said: 'Mr Mandela, what is wrong with you? Don't you hate us?' He just laughed: 'Love your enemy,' he said, 'it will ruin his reputation!' He's right; we're ruined by his goodness. I am delighted to be of service to him as his unofficial Afrikaans hostess, as well as diplomatic troubleshooter. He sometimes rings me in the middle of the night and asks me to read him an Afrikaans poem by Ingrid Jonker, the poet who walked into the sea there by Sea Point. Does he think that maybe she was trying to walk across to Robben Island to see him? I'm sure she was. We will never truly appreciate what this man has done for us. Unless we go back and remember our fear of black majority rule in those terrible days of darkness. Nothing terrible has happened. In fact, very little has changed for the worse, only the better. Viva Mandela!

Memory   Those who cannot remember the past are condemned to repeat it.

Memoirs   A memoir is how one remembers one's own life; while an autobiography is history and has to be accurate!

National Party   I am a member of the National Party. Unlike so many today, I am not ashamed to say so. Yes, I know terrible things were done in our name. I don't know what they were, but I'm sorry. In fact, I'm sorry for everything, even apartheid. Apartheid was a silly little experiment that failed. We are very sorry for apartheid. We promise we won't do it again. But the National Party is now open to all races. People queue up to join: whites to the right, blacks to the left, coloureds in the middle; while the Indians fax through their cheques. And if needs be, I will lead the National Party to Victory in the 1999 elections (see *Death Penalty*).

New South Africa   A now famous phrase to describe where we are today. Ironically it was uttered by all the former Afrikaner leaders at one or other stage of their reigns:

Dr Malan said it when the National Party took control of the country in 1948. Adv. Strydom said it when he took control of the National Party. Dr Verwoerd said it as we became a Republic in 1961. John Vorster said it as terrorists were being hanged in Pretoria. P.W. Botha said it after the Tricameral Parliament was sworn in. F.W. mentioned it as he announced the freeing of the ANC and Mandela. Mandela never stops using it to describe something that has ceased to be that new in 1997.

Naidoo, Jay A vibrant, passionate Indian who was first Minister without Portfolio in charge of the RDP. He lost that when the RDP was stolen. Having promised us one million houses in five years (or was that five houses in a million years?) he is now in charge of Post and Telecommunications. In short, our post is the most expensive and unreliable in the world and our television the worst and now bankrupt. But don't blame Jay; blame apartheid!

Nightmares What I now remember as having been part of my life in the past and is now part of the problem in the present!

Opposition A lazy politician's heaven. If only we in the National Party knew what fun it would be! Because now we are in opposition, for the first time since 1948! What bliss! No need to take reponsibility for anything, except the need to complain. We can now stand at the bottom of the moral high ground humbly and watch the ANC besport themselves in the great temples of power, up on the Olympus of

Democracy. And then watch them come headfirst down the foofie slides of scandal: here comes Winnie, here comes Allan, there goes Bantu. Step aside for Dr Zuma! The poor ANC now looks at our position with intense longing. So much easier being outside the tent pointing in, than inside pointing out. Lyndon Johnson had a cruder way of putting it, but then he was from Texas.

Opinions Something we were denied for so many years thanks to that damned apartheid! It was just outright dangerous, if not subversive, to have an opinion. It was mostly negative. There was a government in Pretoria that had an opinion and handed it down in the shape of laws. But democracy is different. It only exists because of opinion, for or against. Now usually those 'for' win. It's very inconvenient, because it means you have to be sure of an opinion at all times! You must also be confident enough to voice it, in spite of negative reactions at the workplace or round the tea table. And you must be brave enough to change your opinion, when you realise you are wrong, or meet someone with a better opinion. This new craze called Political Correctness is an opinion which levels out most other opinions, but that's to be found under PC.

Overseas Overseas was once anywhere where people didn't speak and understand Afrikaans. Sometimes even Natal was Overseas. Overseas was where communists and the English lived. It was always a threat to us Afrikaners, because if you managed to go overseas, you came back changed. Apartheid could never be the same again. Now overseas is next door. The world is so small; the neighbours are now immigrants.

Optimism Something I have been accused of by those who are terminal pessimists. If I cannot believe that for every negative, there is a positive, I see no point in even carrying on with this sentence! I have always believed that positive energy leads to positive action; negativism can only create another black hole. Divorce, anger, lies, bitterness, war, revenge, hatred, greed and all the other things that make you sick don't help to make the world a better place. Believing in a second chance is reflected in South Africa today. That's an optimistic result of a pessimistic premise! They promised us a bloody revolution; instead we won the World Cup!

Off the record The most chilling phrase politicians can use. It means: what you're about to hear is true. If you publish it you're dead. If you repeat this conversation your family will be killed. If you remember what I'm to say, we'll just deny it. And then kill you!

Politics Politics always has two sides – and a fence. It is the art of getting votes from the poor and money from the rich, by promising to protect each from the other.

Political Correctness The most absurd phrase to describe an impossible dream. Politics is always incorrect, because it is corrupt. To be politically correct in the old South Africa was to subscribe to apartheid, to treat your servants like kaffirs and to believe that you were the chosen people. That today is the opposite of political correctness. So it goes to show: you're only as correct as your politics is powerful.

Power The aphrodisiac that has turned mice into men; men into monsters; monsters into legends and legends into history. Anyone can create it by making the next person use the word in fear.

Pets We've always had animals around the house. My daughter loves cats; my son De Kock small dogs. Izan had a Rottweiler that ate B-J's cat and De Kock's poodle. My husband Hasie has an old cat called Helen. She sleeps in his bed and they are inseparable. Pik and I used the word 'pets' as a nickname for our neanderthal security guards during the days when we both needed protection against personal attack. Those days are over. No more pets who break wind in art galleries and then say 'Sorry, Tannie'!

People The People. Where would we be without them. So much has been said in their name; so much done on their behalf. All in vain. If people cared as much as they complain, if they stood together and shared a commitment, imagine what a society they could create. Sadly this only seems to happen negatively: Germany in the '30s; South Africa in the '60s. Sometimes I look around the world, at the pollution and the dirt, at the poverty and the violence, and I hear myself sigh: pity about people.

Parliament The seat of government and the place where

you could have a nice meal in peace once. That was the old days when the dining-room was a sanctuary. No noise, no journalists, no people, no putu-pap and wors. Just us and bobotie. From 1948 to 1994, Parliament was the National Party Club. We had some opposition in the form of the United Party, then Progressive Party, Progressive Reform Party and the Democratic Party. Ja, they all pretended well and it was a joy being part of that parliamentary clique. Our real opposition was locked up on Robben Island. In Parliament we went through all the motions of democracy: debates, committees, questions, discipline and concern. As a wife of an MP I would spend hours in Hasie's office doing his correspondence. Or just hanging around the powder room talking to the other wives. We would dress up and wear pretty hats and sit up in the public galleries trying to pull faces at the opposition and make them laugh. While our husbands ruled the land, we made up the rules: what to wear, where to wear it, whom to invite. Of course Parliament sat in Cape Town for six months and then we all had to pack up and travel to Pretoria for the recess. What a business! But what a treat to put the packing in the hands of Hasie's staff (later Pik assisted us) and get on the Blue Train for that luxurious ride to the Transvaal. Then after six months in Pretoria, we'd pack it all up and back to Cape Town we would go! They are now discussing the possibility of moving the whole Parliament permanently away from Cape Town. They say for financial reasons. Well, either to Pretoria, Gauteng or Bloemfontein could save some money every six months. But I don't know why they bother. It's too late! Parliament is already moving, day by day, bit by bit.

One day the fax machine, the next day the computer, then the heaters, then the taps.

Parenthood I have three children, and it was my priority to look after them while my husband went about his political career. I can't understand women who want children and then divert their energies into a career. Parenthood is a career, and a full-time job too! My sister and I never had parents in the true sense of the word. Yes, we had a mother and there was a man who called himself our father. But they were always somewhere else. We had to grow up with our maid. I was determined this would never happen with my children. The maid was there, yes, but only to help me. She would bath the children, feed them, put them to bed, wash up and walk the dogs. I would end the day exhausted, but happy. I loved being a parent.

Paraguay For many years this small obscure South American republic was a last-ditch homeland for many of us Afrikaners. We expected the worst, knowing that apartheid would only last as long as we believed in it. And truly, very few of us could with a straight face (see *Apartheid*). The conventional wisdom was: there would be a revolution from within and an invasion from without and we would flee to Paraguay! So we bought farms and started sending tins of tuna over in military aircraft, just in case. But look what happened? The revolution was led by F. W. de Klerk, the leader of the National Party Government! The invasion by the US to support the poor blacks never took place, because South Africa had no oil! Nelson Mandela was released and smiled at us and spoke Afrikaans – and Paraguay had a coup and got rid of that horrible Nazi Stroessner. So there would've been no one to welcome us anyway! Funny how things turn out.

Pollution The result of civilization, development, expansion, growth and prosperity. Too many gases in the air, too much smoke, too few trees, and people, people, people …

Pope At first I was told by my mother (see *Mother*) that the Pope was the Anti-Christ and I believed her, looking at pictures of popes in their horrible red dresses and funny hats. But then I went overseas with the Bothas to show them that the world was round (see *World*) and we went to Rome. It was very beautiful, if somewhat ruined. Probably all those American tourists. The Vatican is where the Pope lives with all the nuns and we went and looked at his place. He has a chapel where Michelangelo worked. Silly. We walked right through the Sistine Chapel and saw nothing. Then we heard back in Pretoria that he had painted the ceiling! Heaven knows why the ceiling! You're supposed to look up! How were we to know? Must go back one day and look again, this time up! The Pope turned out to be very nice. Friendly and quite good-looking. Pity he's a Catholic, but no one's perfect. He once was forced to land at Jan Smuts Airport on his way to Lesotho because of bad weather. And this after he had sworn not to ever set foot in SA during apartheid! It shows: never say never! Pik went to meet him and had breakfast with the Pope in the VIP lounge! The Pope didn't even kiss the ground. He knew how many blacks walked there without shoes on!

Politically motivated crime Can we be serious here for a moment? What monster have we unleashed into the vocabulary of the mass murderer? It started when, during negotiations, two convicted killers were freed from the death cell: Barend Strydom, who during a sunny lunchbreak on Strydom Square in Pretoria, shot and killed over a dozen innocent blacks at random. With a smile on his face! He was freed as his actions were 'politically motivated'. Then to be fair, the ANC's Robert McBride was released for the same reason. He had merely put a bomb in a student bar and killed a handful of innocent white teenagers. The Truth Commission is sorting out politically-motivated actions from the criminally-motivated crimes. South Africa has the highest crime rate in the world, purely because there is no punishment (see *Death Penalty*). The cut-off date for amnesty is being moved so fast that crime can't keep up. If murders can be deemed politically-motivated and therefore excusable, then Adolf Hitler, Joseph Stalin, Pol Pot, Idi Amin and most killers of the innocent are arguably innocent. All crime is politically motivated. This horrible loophole will become the noose round the neck of all democrats very soon.

Psychiatrist I have met a few in the last few weeks. It seems the world's most eminent psychiatrists have come to South Africa to study us! Isn't that funny? They've not come for the wild animals, or the views. Just to look at us ordinary normal South Africans and try and fathom how much trauma and stress we can take before we snap? I tell them all they're crazy. We're fine in South Africa! There's nothing wrong with an eight-foot wall, electrified fences, a moat with crocodiles, landmines on the lawn, rottweilers and pit-bull watchdogs, security guards, bars on the windows, panic buttons, handguns, rifles, AK47s and poison gas to defend your seaside bungalow.

Potjiekos Pik Botha's speciality. He has made this concoction of leftovers in the kitchen with success throughout Africa, through France and Italy, through the United Kingdom, into Greenland, Alaska, the United States, Australia, Brazil and Madeira. Everyone loves it.

Pretoria The capital of the Republic of South Africa. It was then and still is. We all thought the ANC would insist on moving the capital to Soweto. After all, wasn't Soweto the centre of the revolution? But no no no! They also want the perks of power. They are now all in the Union Buildings, using the same offices our people had, the same fridges for their champagne and the same garages for their new Mercedes cars and BMWs. The façade of government has not changed at all: just the noses are flatter and some cheeks slightly coloured. But business as usual in Pretoria, with civil servants being civil to their former servants, now their bosses. Amandla!

Perfume I have always said: a woman is not a woman without a perfume. I could never find one I liked and I tried them all. Some attracted mosquitos and the wrong men, others infuriated police dogs. So I now have a special blend made for me in Paris, France. A soft, alluring presence that is pertinent, while also being private. It has a French name with Afrikaans echoes: 'Jeau 'Mour!'

Plastic surgery Something I have never had the time, nor the courage to have done. I keep a small bottle filled with silver coins as a down payment for the day I think a bit of plastic in my face will improve my inner strength. But till now, I really don't mind looking 51 and being 61. As for the rest of me, Hasie doesn't really take much notice, while Pik always insists that we keep the lights off. But I'll take a rain check on this: if I need some, I have the best plastic surgeon in the world. He's already turned chalk into cheese (see *De Klerk*).

PAC The Pan Africanist Congress. The radical left-of-centre-of-the-rabble; a political party that caused so many of us fear and worry with their election slogans: Kill the Boer/Kill the Farmer! It led to their downfall as well. Today the PAC is nothing more than a fax machine without paper. Two notable members are Patricia de Lille and Bennie Alexander.

Queen Elizabeth II Either the monarch ruling the United Kingdom or a large cruise liner. The monarch visited South Africa recently where she had a lovely time being treated to Amandla-courtesy by the Comrades: Tokyo Sexwale put his arm round her! The new Mayor of Cape Town, dressed casually and without his chain at the official reception for the Queen, said he only wore his chain for important occasions! And a radio reporter called her 'Queen Elizabeth the Eleventh' and her husband 'the Duck of Eedenburg'! The poor woman has no charisma other than her jewellery and her reputation as a parent. She leads a terrible family of strange-looking boys with eyes too close together and a girl who looks like a horse. Queen Elizabeth was the mother-in-law to Princess Diana and so will not be easily forgotten.

Queer Not a nice English word. I use it to describe things that perplex me, but have been badly misunderstood. It is really irritating: now those 'types' have hijacked two perfectly good English words and made them their own: queer and gay!

Quotes Something one always gets wrong. Or attributes words to someone who never said them. Or one just makes them up. A favourite Afrikaans phrase has always been 'soos N.P. van Wyk Louw gesê het': and then one says just what comes to mind. No one knows the difference and everyone is impressed! And so instead of giving facts, pretend to quote the unspeakable and not take the blame for saying it out straight!

Quantas Airlines Australia's airline that has taken so many of our qualified people away into self-imposed exile. The IQ of both our countries went up! Strange place, this Australia. But I can see that we have a lot in common. While it was founded by convicts, South Africa will be ended by convicts!

Qwagga This word is always found in the Q-section of any A to Z. It's also a South African animal: a hybrid between a zebra and a horse. I see no reason for its creation and sense it was mistake. Like the Japanese.

Religion One day when I get to Heaven, there are two people I want to hit. Hard. One is Hendrik Verwoerd for having led us down the segregated garden path. The other one is Calvin. And I don't mean the boy who designs jeans. The creator of Calvinism is responsible for all my fears, all my prejudice, all my so-called arrogance, and all my nightmares. In a nutshell: my hell! Thanks to Calvinism, I never spoke out when my instinct screamed RUN! I never questioned when my better judgement whispered LEAVE NOW! Never gave one thought to the obvious, even though the obvious was dying in front of my eyes. Of course I believe in God (see *God*). How could I be what I am if it wasn't for Him? But what He is and where, is a secret He won't divulge. And frankly nor will I. Although to give you a clue: he is to be reached on http://www.co.god

Racism Racism is the virus of the '90s, the AIDS of civilized life. As natural to each person as the blue eyes and brown hair that make his friend different. Race is such a stupid word. Racism is bad; individualism is good. So let's concentrate on that (see *Individualism*). But are we all racists? Look, I don't like the English for obvious reasons. That does not make me a racist. It makes me anti-English. I don't like the Jews, because I don't understand their blind belief that they are always right. Does that make me anti-semitic? No!

I just don't like Jews! I can't stand cheeky blacks. Polite blacks I like. Some of my best friends have black friends. But these cheeky blacks? I can't stand them! Especially the American ones! Does this make me a white supremacist? No, it shows I have taste. Indians get on my nerves, because they are so ingratiating. Italians smell of garlic. French are rude. Americans are stupid and loud. No, Greeks are loud; the Americans are just stupid. Irish are dazed. Dutch are fat. Germans are all over the place and look so silly you can't help but laugh. Slanty-eyed people just make me read the book by Nostradamus, where he says they'll rule the world in 2000. So when I see one, I tend to swerve my car just in case I can save the world. So basically I hate everyone! Including Afrikaners, who are the most stupid lot of losers I have ever met in my life! But that doesn't make me a racist. Just a good and very normal white South African!

Radio After reading, there is nothing in the world that has given me better pictures than on the television or films, than radio. I have listened to radio as long as I can remember, because we only got television in the mid-seventies. How lucky we were! Those serials and plays and voices, all became huge realities in my mind. An earthquake and the birth of a baby, a car chase and a storm. Eating, drinking, laughing and sleeping. Singing and dancing. Being famous. Being someone. All thanks to radio. The greatest way to get into someone's mind! And staying there!

Relaxing Everyone wants to know: Evita, how do you relax? I don't use that word, 'relax'. It has images of floppy limbs and a tongue lolling out of the mouth. Diversity in action is my answer. Plan your life. Make lists. Decide your priorities. Empty your mind of trivia and detail. And once everything is on a list or in a filofax, then you can concentrate on what needs your attention. By moving your attention from a new grandchild to a potroast is relaxation. Leaving a meeting and then having a bath is relaxation. You don't need to go on holiday. It's just too much hard work. You just need to change gear. Relaxing also means not thinking about anything. Sit on a chair and stare at nothing for ten minutes. Bliss. Until you see how badly the maid has dusted the stinkwood furniture!

Ramaphosa, Cyril   A brilliant young manipulator, a charmer and a great trout-catcher! Also a man to watch. He came out of the ranks of the internal struggle and soon helped to write the Constitution. A man of great appeal. I have been seduced by his smile many a time. We have a saying in Afrikaans: 'Stille water, diepe grond – daaronder dans die duiwel rond?' That's Cyril to a T. Rather than go down as a political wannabe, he is now outside politics as the Harry Oppenheimer of Black Empowerment. I'm happy with him outside politics. That's the real world for Cyril, who is a shaker and a mover. If not of our hormones, then of contracts and investments. Keep an eye on him. More to come.

Revolution   I have always loved that funny line: 'the natives are revolting'. Well, they didn't in South Africa, although they often were! We never had a black revolution, we had a white one. We in power stopped our power! Like turkeys voting for Christmas, we democratically toppled ourselves. We opened the door and said to the enemy on the barricade: 'Come in and have some tea!' I just think we learnt the wrong words in Xhosa. We probably said: 'Come in and help yourself!'

Rands and Cents The rand is becoming a cent. It is reputedly a clever ploy by the communist in charge, the Minister of Finance, Trevor Manuel. To prevent politicians from stealing taxpayers' money! By devaluing the rand to that extent – R7 plus to one pound? – means that if some elected felon steals R300 million, all they can bank in Switzerland is just $42.22c! But it worries me that the world's economy is all digital and ours is still Manuel!

Rugby Thank heavens for sport! And there is nothing more healing and gracious than a rugby match. I was brought up on rugby. It drove me crazy. There were times when I wanted something else on a Saturday afternoon! But now, when Pik and I need to relax and hide from the necessity of licking each other's wounds, we watch rugby. Granted, sometimes in videos of old Springbok matches. But today's Mandela Amabokoboko are also wonderful. As always we must leave a fly in the cream cake: Louis Luyt! Why do we Afrikaners always have to go down to the lowest common demoninator?

Robben Island The prison island in Table Bay, the Alcatraz of Africa, where our present government was trained. Most of them spent years there. Nelson Mandela was there for 20 years and look what an education it gave him! It was so extraordinary there that they can't seem to stay away! Constant dinner parties are given under the pretext of raising money. One wonders what the black youth thinks, seeing former captains of industry under the apartheid regime having a R250 000-a-head dinner with Madiba? Do Jews have barmitzvahs at Belsen? Oh yes, the United Nationas has put Robben Island on a par with Auschwitz and Hiroshima. I'm not so sure. I don't know anyone who spent 20 years in Auschwitz. And I don't know of anyone who came out of Hiroshima and became President! But I suppose Robben Island is everything for everyone. Like democracy.

Sex Sex should be kept to gender. There is too much written and spoken about this biological aberration. I don't intend talking about it for the simple reason that it is unnecessary and impolite. And I don't know how to spell most of those words. Or what they mean! Ask someone else!

State It always felt like the word describing a huge empty box with secure hinges and strong joins, in which you could safely place all your greatest and most fragile treasure: your future and the dreams of your children. Too often one didn't realise that the bottom of the kist was made of crinkle paper. Precious things would fall through and get lost. A state of mind is often a safer place to invest in.

Sanctions Much ado about nothing! How we panicked in the '80s when the world out there announced sanctions against South Africa because of apartheid? But as we got used to the loud noise, we realized how flimsy the threats were. The successful sanction meant within hours everything to South Africa stopped: air travel, medicine, telephones, trade, post. Within days the regime would have collapsed. But mercifully most supporters of sanctions did it only for the publicity. Economic sanctions would only work if everyone did it properly. It was a farce (see *Hypocrisy*). Holland wouldn't drink South African wine; they poured it into Spanish bottles and then drank it. Germany exported Mercedes cars via Taiwan and the cars arrived in SA with slanting headlamps. Mighty America wouldn't take our Outspan oranges and Britain would throw them down the toilet. So we sent oranges to Israel where they got the Jaffa stamp and everyone ate them! Ha ha!

Intellectual sanctions meant a cultural boycott: we were not allowed to see the latest plays from the UK or America. Films, yes, but those made too much money to be boycotted. You can imagine what a difference it made to our government policy during the '80s knowing we couldn't see a Harold Pinter play! And the fact that they stopped their own work before we had to openly ban it, helped us immensely. Britain wouldn't let us see their television programmes. So we got all our programmes from America. And today South Africa understands American humour and doesn't have much enjoyment of British jokes or accents. The sports sanctions were the only truly successful boycott: we Afrikaners love seeing balls being kicked. We even were prepared to allow blacks to sit with us. So we killed apartheid for the sake of sport, and not because of sanctions.

Struggle 'The Struggle'. A famous title for a long-running farce. I am so sick of the word 'Struggle'. Everything good happened then during The Struggle; everything bad is blamed on apartheid. I start wondering: where would The Struggle have been if it wasn't for apartheid? Where would those famous people have been if they didn't have the excuse of sitting in overseas universities and colleges and hotels and bars and having their bills paid by the anti-apartheid movement? Where would most of the present-day millionaires in South Africa be without The Struggle and its financial rewards? (See *Boesak*) And who chose the word 'Struggle'? It's ineffectual. You struggle to free a strap trapped under a chair. You battle for freedom. 'The Battle' it should have been called, but no, just a Struggle. A skirmish. And ironically we all now find out that the two great opposing armies of Apartheid and Freedom were made up of amateurs, drunks, liars, hypocrites and fools. They deserved a mere struggle.

Sies A wonderful Afrikaans word that also defies translation. The nearest is 'sis'. It means the sound you make when you feel your foot slide into something soft on the sidewalk. Or if you blow your nose into a tissue and it gives way. Or when someone tells you a joke that makes your eyes water with laughter, but you can't be seen to laugh. Then you say: sies!

Struggle bookkeeping I have to include this remarkable contradiction, as it could only emerge from South Africa. It seems that the reason why much investor cash from bleeding-heart lands like Denmark and Sweden got lost during the last ten years (see *Boesak, Allan*) is not due to theft or embezzlement, but to 'struggle bookkeeping'! It is so outrageous that one actually gives them the benefit of the doubt. Why didn't we think of that too? Apartheid-accounting just doesn't seem right. It sounds wrong!

Slabbert, Van Zyl Formerly the leader of the PFP, this young Afrikaner broke the mould of what we in Government expected from a Leader of the white Opposition. He spoke fluent Afrikaans! He was one of us! At first we brushed him aside as a hippy and a closet communist, but he spoke with such passion and made such sense, that I was even approached to woo him onto our side. I tried nearly everything. I even managed to lure him off on an intimate picnic near Arniston, on a beach with no one in sight. Except the aerial attached to my bodyguard's walkietalkie! But Van just quoted great reams of Afrikaans poetry and put the whole episode in perspective by calling me Tannie! I gave up after that. Slabbert shocked us all by suddenly resigning as Leader of the Opposition. I think he was hoping that his whole party would follow him, so making South Africa the one-party state we were, but pretended otherwise by pointing to our opposition. His party changed their minds. The loss of perks, pensions, salaries and top positions was too much for them. The walkout fizzled to one man leaving. I was sad to see him go, but relieved that he kept his integrity. He still contributes a great deal from the backrooms of political intrigue. He is sadly the wrong colour to lead the land, but has the right mettle to make all the difference. If only he didn't always call me Tannie. 'Skattie' would open up such a new fantasy.

Suzman, Helen For most of the years I went to Parliament with my husband, there was one person who really frightened me. It was Helen Suzman. I used to stare at her, sitting there alone in her bench, the only member of the PFP in Parliament. In fact the only vocal opposition to us in power. I kept wondering what made her do what she did: challenge the most powerful men in the land with facts that no one dared even breathe. She also looked so ordinary. A small housewife? I think not! Once B.J. Vorster called her a 'schnauzer', which is some or other small dog with a sharp-pointed nose. P.W. Botha loathed her. I remember when Verwoerd was murdered by Dimitri Tsafendas (see *Tsafendas*), Botha went crazy and pointed at Helen Suzman accusing her of being part of a plot to kill the Prime Minister! Already then we should have known that P.W. was off his marbles. Helen Suzman pointed the way, not just for us in Government, but to us women. She behaved like the tallest man in a man's world, but never lost her feminine touch. A lethal touch. She survived them all. She is now retired, but never stops lecturing and travelling. I think she likes me; we have had some charming tea and cake together when I was ambassador in Bapetikosweti. I miss her in politics. We need her now more than ever before.

Strydom, J.G. The second Nationalist Prime Minister, after D.F. Malan. I didn't know him at all, but he looked quite nice. I believe he was married to an actress, but divorced her. He even changed his name when he became a politician: the 'y' in Strydom to 'Strijdom'. Why would we be more impressed with a Prime Minister with a Dutch surname? He looked like Stalin without his moustache!

Sun Avoid it! Wear hats and gloves and sunglasses. There is nothing more glorious than a sunny day in South Africa, but watch it from indoors, video it and look at it on television. It's safer for your skin!

Soldier All mothers had one of those in the family during the last twenty years. Some mothers lost sons. Some sons didn't die, but lost their will to live. There are hospital wards still full of half-men, crippled survivors of pointless battles. We were told it was to fight communism, to uphold democracy, to protect Christianity. Rubbish! It was greed and self-interest. Someone gave the orders. I wonder who. (See *Malan, Magnus*)

Satire No, I'm sorry, I have never found this type of thing funny. What is there in politics to make people laugh? Yes, P.W. wagged his finger and licked his lips and looked like a fool, but how can you make a career out of copying that? I've never even been sure what this satire looks like. At least if I recognised it, I could avoid it. They say we had a few of those satirists in the past. I don't think they were that clever. (see *Uys, P-D*). Just desperate and foulmouthed. And now redundant!

SABC The South African Broadcasting Corporation which controlled television and radio from the beginning. We only got TV in the mid-1970s. There was a minister in Vorster's government who called it 'the devil's box'. He was right of course. He said it would mean the end of life as we know it. He was right again! While the SABC was carefully infiltrated with the right people during the Old Regime, it is being restocked with the right, in this case left, people (see *Affirmative Action*). When democracy took over the SABC in 1994 they had a surplus of R40 million. In three years that has become a deficit of R60 million. I don't ever want to say I told you so but what can I say? I told you so!

SAA South African Airways, which bravely during the horrible sanctions years had to fly round the bulge of Africa to the rest of the world. And managed! Recently a new corporate livery took over from the old orange, white and blue. The flying springbok is also no more. Nor is Afrikaans. How we remember those times in foreign lands unloved and unwanted, and reaching the airports, only to see the sad little orange tail with its flying springbok, far in a secluded quarantine corner of the airport? It made one feel so homesick. Now the colours include the new flag hues, and a large golden sun against a red background. Or is it a bullet hole?

South Africa I cannot think of any other country I want to have been born in. It's been through hell and it's come out smiling. It has been given a second chance. It is the most beautiful country in the world. It has in it some of the most generous people in the world. It has the world's youngest and most dynamic democracy. And it has as its leader, Nelson Mandela. What more could we wish for?

Sister For years I pretended my sister Baby had died. I lied. Baby is younger than me and never stops rubbing it in. 3 years younger! Not, as she now tells the press, 13 years younger! She came with me and Mimi to Vienna, where I left her when I went back to SA. Baby got a job as a waitress in a bar there, 'Der Blaue Engel'. There was an old cabaret singer called Zarah Leander who introduced Baby to an older German man, Joachim von Kellermann. Baby fell in love with him and married him. Only then did she realise that he had been a Nazi commander of one of the camps during the war. As a result everyone wanted to put him on trial. So in order for him to stay hidden comfortably, my sister, now known as Bambi, started life as a stripper and a sex object. Throughout Europe she danced naked and also, I am told, did a sexual act with a donkey called Fritz! Then she and her husband managed to get to Paraguay (see *Paraguay*), where Kellermann became Minister of War in the Government of Alfredo Stroessner. When General Kellermann died a few years ago, Bambi came back to SA with his ashes in an urn, looking for a burial place for this horrible dead Nazi. She is still here, doing cabarets during which she belittles Afrikaans culture and calls us all Nazis. At least we didn't marry them! She should talk! We have no communication at all. She has two children somewhere overseas. And a young man who is her secretary. Someone told me she runs a brothel in Paarl. I don't believe it. Not in Paarl!

Sorry A horrible little word. Too little, always too late. But being an Afrikaner means never having to say: sorry!

Self-confidence Some regard too much of it as arrogance. I see too little of it as irritating and expecting hand-outs and constant help. If you can't have the confidence to trust your motives and your abilities, why should anyone else bother? Great examples and inspirations are Imelda, Margaret and that Madonna.

Sport Where would we in South Africa be without it? The god of all Afrikaans men. Rugby ruled. SA radio and television on a Saturday is just sport. I am so sick of it, I can scream. But then my mother would always sigh with relief as the men rushed out of the house to their various sporting matches. It gave her peace and quiet. I suppose she's right. Sport has again taken the forefront in the new SA. We won the Rugby World Cup in Newlands. There was no alternative to winning. The other side was paralysed by Nelson Mandela, coming on the field wearing the No. 6 Springbok jersey and cap, and shaking hands with the poor All Blacks. The old witchdoctor! We are also tops in soccer (see *Bafana*) and various Olympic sports. Or we were yesterday. A lot can change when a ball is wrongly kicked! And as we all know, you're only as good as your last match!

Superstition I don't walk under ladders, because I've heard stories of paint falling over your furcoat. I don't mind black cats, having learnt to handle anything black as an occupational hazard. I have very few superstitions, except the ones I cannot mention because of what will happen to me if I do.

School I hated it and was so glad it was over. All I learnt was to hide from the other girls. Yes, I was fat! Yes, my hair was very 'kroes'! Yes, my teeth stuck out! And yes, I was top of my class, because I knew the principal had a fat coloured girlfriend. Once he knew I knew, I passed with flying colours.

Thatcher, Baroness Margaret Formerly British Prime Minister over and over again; now Real Legend and Most Irritating British Politician in Britain, but Saint in the USA and South Africa. Yes, I sometimes wonder where we whites would be without her. She was our one friend during the years when the world had its bitter sanctions against us. She alone refused to throw our Outspan oranges in the toilet! She alone fought for the right to drink KWV wine! She made bad friends in the Commonwealth, even an enemy of her own Queen, all on our behalf. We kept asking ourselves: why? Now we know. It was in exchange for political asylum for her son, Mark. He is now living in Cape Town. She named him Mark after the German currency, because she had no faith in the British pound. I saw Maggie just before Xmas last year at the Pick 'n Pay in Constantia. She'd come out to spend Xmas with her son and his family. It was difficult being certain it was she, because all the women in Constantia look like Margaret Thatcher. But in the carpark one of the skollies tried to mug her and she beat him up with her handbag! It was the Iron Lady all right, still with half a brick in her bag. Princess Diana's fat brother is also living in Cape Town, by the way. Earl Spencer. So now we have Mark and Spencer! The first person I introduced F.W. de Klerk to after making him President was Prime Minister Thatcher (see *De Klerk*). She always liked him. She said they had a very satisfactory exchange of views. He would come to Downing Street with his views and leave with hers.

Theatre Pik used to be a spearcarrier in old National Theatre plays. He's now a part-time spearcarrier in present National Party productions! Oh, I used to enjoy the theatre until I realised how irrelevant it was. And that I could never get a job as an actress. And anyway, who wants to swop a world stage for a small platform in a cold, dark, empty auditorium? I think I made the right choice.

Truth and Reconciliation Initials: TRC. The recital of the writing on the wall. With details and tears! The most terrible stories have been told to the Commission and it makes us cringe. How could we have been responsible for all that? Murder, torture, death? Of course, you just have to look at those who admit to doing these things. Criminal faces and cauliflower ears! Look like fired rugby players! Obvious felons. And now they speak as if they represent all Afrikanerdom? No, no, no! We Afrikaners did not do such things. We would never do the things these criminals admit doing! And get caught! I suppose the fact that the TRC is not out to punish anyone is a Godsend. We should make use of it before the backlash starts. At the moment widows and orphans of those killed by apartheid power just want to know who did it. To forgive them! Soon it will be more practical and bloody. Will we be able to get away with it after all? I can't believe we have so far! Somewhere there must be a snag.

Tutu, Desmond Former Archbishop and once a major meddlesome priest in the political life of white South Africa and soon the most irritating anti-apartheid mosquito round the ears of the white apartheid elephant. But since I realised that we were sort of wrong and he was maybe right, I have grown to respect him. He's a good man, in spite of being Anglican and black. And he likes me! In fact, when I meet him, because he's so small, I have to bend forward so that he can kiss my hand. And then he looks down my front! *Stoute kabouter*. Of course, it's OK for him to do that because he's Anglican. It's the Catholics who go straight to hell. Desmond Tutu is now sadly ill with cancer. Being so closely involved with the terrible facts of the horrors of the past can't be helping his health. We have been so lucky to have been blessed with two of the best: Tutu and Madiba. What did we do to deserve them? And when they're gone, who will look after us? I'm really quite nervous ...

Toyi-Toyi A silly dance that is reputed to be the war dance of true liberation. Polony! It looks like elementary Zulu aerobics. It's visible everywhere. Whenever blacks

83

decide not to work, because they're lazy, overfed, or just drunk, they toyi-toyi for Africa and appear on world television and everyone says: 'Look, the rhythm! Look, the dancing! The music! The will of the people'. (Of course, those who say that are just whites without rhythm!) If I see any more fat nurses toyi-toyi on TV in the streets, while their patients die in the wards, I will scream! For 3 years these nurses have been toyi-toying! And it's not working! They're not losing weight. *Hulle sterte bly nog net so groot!*

Talent Too many people are impressed by mere talent as the end-all. I demand talent as the beginning, as the oxygen before we breathe! Without basic talent, get out of the traffic! If you have talent, learn to drive. Fast!

Tsafendas, Dimitri Again I refuse to take the blame here. While Hasie was in Parliament as MP for Laagerfontein, I was stuck as a mere parliamentary wife in that horrible little house in Acacia Park. I decided to renovate: throw out all that horrible yellow-wood flooring and put in nice linoleum, as well as repaint the walls. But who would do it for me? I didn't trust those Cape Coloured who were all so cheeky and would talk back in Afrikaans without teeth, making the language sound like a dialect! So I asked Hasie to find me someone else. He said a secretary in the Ministry of Justice, John Vorster's office, suggested a Greek who was without work. I don't like Greeks because their hair is so oily and they break plates, but I like Coloureds less. So we employed him. Tsafendas was his name, a horrible tall man with curly oily hair and mad. He kept talking about a worm! Imagine that!

Anyway he started painting the house. A mess everywhere! What should have been a yellow wall, ended up green; pink looked blue! Eventually my mother said the smell of his paint would get into my fresh koeksisters and lose me the title of Best Koeksister Baker of the Year (See *Koeksisters*). So Hasie went back to Vorster's office and it was suggested that this Dimitri get a job in Parliament as a temporary messenger. This suited me fine, because his painting was horrible. But Parliament in those days didn't automatically feed the temps, like it does today. So we packed a little lunch box for Dimitri – koeksisters, boerewors, droëwors, potato salad and a nice Granny Smith apple. Of course, my mother, obsessed with hygiene, insisted that Dimitri take a small fruitknife to peel the apple. What can I tell you! He went to Parliament as mad as he was, got things terribly mixed up, wanted to peel the apple, but peeled the PM instead! Yes, Tsafendas stabbed Dr. Hendrik Verwoerd to death with my fruitknife! Stupidly he didn't stab Vorster at the same time, or for good measure, use the Golden Mace to beat P.W. Botha's brains out! Imagine, we could have got rid of three Broeders with one Greek! But the reality was this: Verwoerd was dead, thanks to my fruit-knife! So now B. J. Vorster was Prime Minister (see *Vorster*). When I saw my poor little fruit-knife again, he was cleaning his nails with it and staring at me with what I thought was a smile. It wasn't. Now looking back, I feel I should take credit for something, but I don't know what it is.

Tourists Now they're coming from all over the world to a democratic South Africa, just to be raped, robbed and murdered by the potential voters who roam the streets in search of another chance for 'affirmative shopping'! (See *Stealing*) African-Americans are constantly in tears, rediscovering their roots and sniffing: 'Oprah was right!' Many tourists come from Sydney, Perth and Melbourne to see where all those doctors and dentists and vets come from! British tourists look more like refugees, and most of them are ex-South Africans coming back in disguise, just in case someone sees them in the supermarket and says: 'Oh, you've come back to South Africa? Did you fail overseas?' The German tourists are the funniest, because they look so silly with their sandals, white socks, funny short pants and countless cameras. I think they go to a special shop in Hamburg to get the costume. The reason so many Germans come to South Africa is probably to see how we got away with apartheid.

University When I was small we were always told: go to university and get a degree to fall back on! Never get a degree to fall forward on! What a terrible example of the South African retreat-mentality. No matter what your dream, it will be a flop. So get a degree to fall back on. You'll hate every minute of your life, but you will have security. Really? De Kock says the most-used phrase among our graduates today is: 'Chips? Or baked potato?'

Uys, P-D A third-rate comedian who couldn't make it as a playwright and then found out how susceptible our society is to obscene language, and to men wearing women's clothing. He has made his name making fun of me on the stages of the world. I have been tempted to sue him for libel, but then as Pik has pointed out, 'don't give him the publicity!' We allowed this comic to carry on making fun of us during the apartheid years. To show how democratic we were. Besides the jails were full. Now that apartheid is gone and with it all the material that gave him so much to say, this comic is repeating tired old jokes and not looking like me at all! He's too fat, too short, too unimaginative. And I never use the word 'skattie'! But he has good legs. Not as good as me, but good...

United Nations A group of useless committees, subcommittees, secretaries and secretary-generals, who spend millions asking for more millions, and waste hours doing nothing. Supposedly to keep the world free of war, the UN just encourages nationalism and expansionist dreams of those countries that should never have qualified for statehood in the first place. Bring back the colonial structures, where like children in a classroom, there is a teacher! And homework! And punishment for being naughty. The UN tries to do it all in the playtime!

Viva A word the Struggle took over to mean something positive. The mindless masses shout 'Viva' at the smallest provocation. I think they think it means 'Long Life'. But they usually all shout it before necklacing an innocent bystander (see *Winnie*).

Voting Either you have the vote or you don't. If you don't, you lose your life to get it. If you have it, often you lose your freedom by not using it. Either way, it is the most dangerous and exciting weapon to put in anyone's hands.

Violence It has taken over from sport and recreation in South Africa as the one thing that everyone is aware of and can do nothing about. It is blamed on apartheid like bad weather and fleas, but basically means crime does pay. More than that, it has even become an investment. There is only one way to combat violence. With more violence! Until we have got rid of all the perpetrators of violence. Then we can settle down to a normal life of law and order, in other words, civilized violence!

Voortrekkers See *Great Trek*.

Victim Slowly but surely we have become a nation of professional victims. We now stand in the ruins of what we have destroyed with our hands open and expect handouts. The word 'demand' has become the alternative to the need to 'earn'. Compared to other emerging countries like China where every inch of land is being cultivated, South Africans don't plant for tomorrow. We do not invest for a future. We just expect someone else to do it for us. Mistake number one!

Vorster, Balthazar John The cold, callous Minister of Justice who became Prime Minister after the murder of Verwoerd. While only 13th in line, he soon turned South Africa into a police state. An unsmiling brutal man, he did not like me at first. But after I stood up to him, we became friends right to the end, when sad and pathetic he shuffled out of his office in disgrace, a victim of P.W. Botha's vicious poison politics (see *The Information Scandal*). He died virtually forgotten in Port Elizabeth and wanted to be buried privately. But P.W. turned it into a victory rally for himself (see *Botha, P.W.*).

White Not a colour in the rainbow. Nor is black or brown. So what does this Rainbow Nation mean?

Wine We have some of world's best vineyards and some wonderful wines. I am very proud that there are two wines named after me: Evita Blanc and Evita Noir.

Water My most interesting public appearance in this new South Africa was when they renamed the Hendrik Verwoerd Dam. Prof Kader Asmal, Minister of Water Affairs, invited me as an old Free State meisie to do the honours. It was a bizarre experience: a blinding hot day on the surreal concrete walls of that great erection, making speeches to an audience of deeply drunk local coloureds all celebrating something. I wore the ethnic outfit I'd bought from Winnie Mandela at her garage sale, held to pay for the divorce from Nelson. Kader and I cut the ribbon and renamed it the Gariep Dam. It could have been worse. Thank heavens the little dam named after me somewhere in former Bapetikosweti has been dry so long no one can find it to rename it!

Winnie Like Churchill she is known by that name.

Nomsamo Winifred Madikizela-Mandela is her new combination, which is practical for court appearances. By the time the long name is called, she is already in the car on the way home. Now the ex-Mrs Mandela, Winnie is the bounce-back champion of the ANC. No sooner has she disappeared in disgrace, than she suddenly makes another comeback. She has been convicted for the Stompie kidnapping, although not for his killing. I have little to add here, other than to say that after what we put her through for those 27 years, anything is nearly excusable. Imagine: a husband in jail who could be released at any time? Then those terrible years in exile in the OFS? That shack in Brandfort's location? And Brandfort is like Las Vegas without adverts or hotels! Horrible. Then Winnie ignores her banning order and ends up in Soweto, the darling of the liberal world and the itchy thorn in our side. She makes us cross wherever she can. She even gathers a gang of thugs round her and calls them her Football Team. And then the Stompie Affair? Look, if you end up without a husband at that fragile middle-age, while still beautiful, and desirable? And find yourself in a jacuzzi with 15 naked soccer players? Any woman's hormones would go on a route march! And then a small boy runs in and spoils it by saying: 'Mama, there's someone on the phone?' I would've also beaten him to death! Keep an eye on Winnie. She's bound to put her foot in it again and be disgraced before the end of the year. But she'll be back soon afterwards. And in the 1999 election Winnie will be a major candidate for the Presidency. She doesn't call herself the 'Black Evita' for nothing!

War A state in which I think I and the rest of South Africa spent most of our lives. And who won?

Walls When the one in Berlin came down I was quite angry. I was on my way to Germany to offer to buy it, so we could put it round Soweto! But it was already broken. And yet the wall went within. The people of the liberated east still regard themselves as different. Ask any Ossie. It's all so much like apartheid. Officially it ceased to exist, but in the mind of millions it's still there. The walls round the homes of Gauteng symbolise this. They get higher every time an innocent is murdered and the guilty go unpunished.

Women Behind ever successful man is a clever woman. Behind every successful woman is a man who knows his place without having to be told.

Xhosa The second largest tribe in South Africa. Most of the ANC have their roots in the Xhosa heritage. Traditionally they don't get on very well with the Zulus (see *Zulus*), but maybe this was just part of old apartheid propaganda. Voortrekkers and Boers had many bloody wars with the Xhosa. Even the British Settlers of 1820 changed their minds about the Noble Savage when they came face to face with the Xhosa. Today it's obvious who won.

X-Rated Now there is freedom of speech in South Africa, in other words no censorship, even though there is still a censorboard and censors drawing salaries. Now pornography is also freely available. I don't like it at all, but I am no longer in the position to pick up a phone and get a Minister excited enough to do something about it. But I resent taking my grandchildren to the corner café and seeing that horrible *Hustler* magazine on the same shelf where they get their little packets of nice sweets. Sies and sis! These disgusting degrading magazines should be kept on the top shelf in their plastic bags, so that the dominee and the censor need to ask for the ladder to get to them!

Zulu The most powerful tribe in South African History. Black tribe, that is. Based mainly in Natal, they have been led for some years by Chief Buthelezi (see *Buthelezi*) and King Goodwill Zwelithini. The Zulu homeland was never realised under apartheid, although Buthelezi as Chief Minister enjoyed the perks of power without paying any dues. Now he is in the Government of National Unity as Minister for Home Affairs, while at the same time leading the IFP. KwaZulu–Natal is the home of most Zulus, although you will find far too many in Johannesburg and even one or two in the Cape. Don't ever mix them up with Xhosas! It's like asking a Swede if he was an Italian! Zulus are not to be trifled with; they slaughter first and laugh last. My mother always said there were only two things one could do to a Zulu: put him in government or in a grave. No compromise.

Zimbabwe Formerly Rhodesia. The first white homeland to fall in that domino-principle of democratic downgrading in Africa. Ian Smith declared UDI and presented us with the most perfect buffer state to the North. We supported Smith's

Rhodesia until we saw the writing on his wall. Even from the distance we were it was the end of white domination there. Ian Smith couldn't resist driving the angry British even madder, but eventually democracy had its way thanks to the lowest common denominator and today Robert Mugabe is still the President. I am told his view of democracy is very African: 'Everyone is free to do as I say!'

Zip A zip is very often the difference between elegance and chaos. How many of us have bent down to kiss a small child and felt one's zip go? When will we learn to dress like real Africans and not Park Avenue matrons? No zips on Winnie: her mouth or her outfit!

Zuma Not the name of a new Ford, but the Minister of Health. Dr Nkosasana Zuma has made her mark already by commissioning *Sarafina 2* and inviting 250 Cuban doctors to South Africa (see *Cuba*). I've met her a few times and she is always very friendly. I wonder sometimes if she's a real doctor, or if she got her doctorate like most of the Broeders did: by sending a R150 cheque to a PO Box in Potchefstroom? Of course, Nelson Mandela won't hear a word against her. When he came out of jail, he had a terrible headache after listening to Van der Merwe jokes in Afrikaans for 27 years. So Mrs Zuma gave him half a Disprin and cured his headache. Now he says she is a medical genius. And she can dance the toyi-toyi.

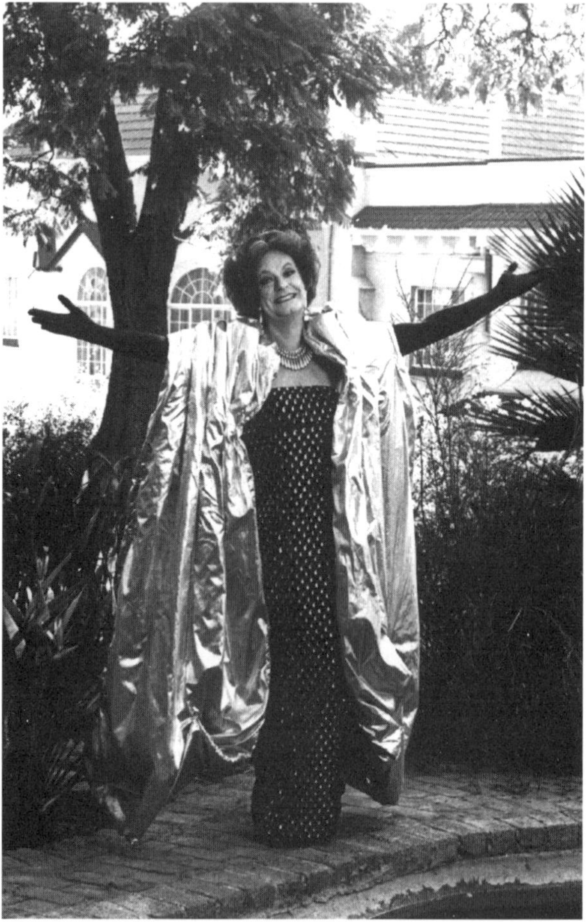